全国普通高等学校优秀教材一等奖 第一版
普通高等教育"十一五"国家级规划教材

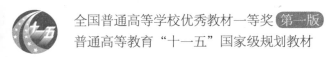

U0095404

总主编 黄源深 虞苏美

Integrated Skills of English

综合英语教程

Zonghe Yingyu Jiaocheng

第三版

主 编 邹为诚

编 者 邹为诚 陈 舒 王世静 张 逸

2

Student's Book
学生用书

高等教育出版社·北京
HIGHER EDUCATION PRESS BEIJING

《综合英语教程》第三版是"国家精品课程"(2005) 项目的主要研究成果之一。此次修订，课题组的老师们在全国十几所高校的协助下，开展了大量的课堂实践研究。在现代外语教学理念的指引下，课题组在题材选择、内容编排、教学设计、练习方法、教学指导等方面都进行了修改，改动幅度较之第二版显著增大。多年来持之以恒的研究和课堂实践使得第三版在课堂教学设计等诸方面都达到了一个新的高度。

第三版教材具有如下特色：

1. 全面注重学习者的真实需要，开发了切合学生实际需要的听、说、读、写任务，更好地把语言知识、语言技能和学习者的认知能力发展综合在一起。

2. 题材选择上符合时代和学习者的实际需要，全书更替的内容达三分之一以上。第三版教材的思想和文化内容，涵盖了当代社会的重要方面，反映了时代的进步和发展，有助于学习者获得地道的语言输入。

3. 第三版教材增强了语言学习的文学性色彩。文学是语言学习和人文修养的最佳手段，其主要困难是如何将文学性有效地渗透在语言学习的过程中，教师如何通过文学作品在宏观和微观两个方面发展学习者的外语能力，同时提高学习者的人文品质修养？第三版教材体现了我们对这些问题的研究。实践表明，根据这些思考和研究所设计的课堂教学具有很好的教学效果。

4. 教学任务的设计更加强调"教学效能"。"教学效能"是综合英语课程研究的核心问题之一，第三版教材的教学设计融合了大批优秀教师的课堂教学经验，教学任务更加有趣生动、训练程度大幅度增加，但并没有额外增加学生的"学习负荷"。

5. 第三版教材的训练栏目设计更加符合课堂教学的实际，为广大学生和教师带来学习和教学两方面的方便，令他们在使用上感到更加得心应手，更加有利于他们发挥自己的特长。

6. 第三版教材配有MP3光盘，凡注有🎧标识的部分均可在光盘中找到相应的录音。

7. 第三版教材配有学习卡，供学生进入四、八级模拟考试平台进行两次免费测试。

《综合英语教程》第三版的出版是全国几十所高等院校英语专业师生共同努力的结果，作为编者，我们希望广大师生能一如既往地支持本教程的完善工作。教程的开发只有起点，没有终点，我们愿意和广大师生一起不断努力，把我国的外语教学课程开发研究推向新的高度。

《综合英语教程》编写组
于华东师范大学
2011年元月

《综合英语教程》第一版问世以来，得到了全国上百所普通高等院校英语专业老师和学生的支持，为我国英语专业基础阶段的教学作出了很大的贡献。随着社会的发展，我国英语专业基础阶段的教学出现了许多变化，为了适应这些变化，编写组于2002年起对本教材进行了全面的修改。第二版充分反映了教师们开展教学实验的结果，修改和删除了一些不受学生和教师欢迎、课堂操作困难或过于机械的项目，增加了课堂效果良好的、有助于促进学生在语言和知识两方面发展的任务和内容，并根据课堂实验重新编写了内容更加丰富的教师用书。

编写组认为，教材的修订不应仅仅是课堂操作层面上的改进，还应反映学科的最新变化，以及当前外语教学领域开展的一些重要变革。

众所周知，在最近5年里，教育界发生了翻天覆地的变化，外语教育也不例外。传统的教学观念、教学手段、学习目的和学习方法都已产生了巨大的变化，其中最突出的是对学生主体的重新认识。教学界重新认识到教师必须根据学生的认知需要、情感需要和语言交流的需要来开展教学，这一原则在第二版教材中有如下体现：

1. 强调"以学生为中心，以教师为主导"的观念。第二版教材在教学活动的设计上，强调从学生已有知识出发，引导学生去探索未知的知识；教师在引导过程中，及时为学生传授语言和知识。

2. 第二版教材强调教材和教师在语言示范方面的共同作用。传统教材以教学材料为主要的语言示范工具，这对学习者的语言习得有极大帮助。但是，这种静止式的语言示范有很大的局限性，它排斥了语言教师的动态语言示范作用，教师无法准确地把握学生语言发展和学生交际需要之间的关系。第二版教材采用"静止式示范 (Single-mode Modeling)"与"动态式示范 (Interactive Modeling)"相结合的模式，强调教师通过语言交流活动，发现学生的交际需要，采用有针对性的"动态语言示范"，创造让学生"顿悟"语言的机会。

3. 第二版教材同时强调语言的"正面"和"负面"输入 (Positive and Negative Input)。语言的"正面输入"指的是教师、教材以及教学活动和环境为学生提供的正确的语言形式，"负面输入"指的是学生在语言活动中得到的有关其语言错误的信息。近年来的研究已经证实，有些语言错误可以随着语言的发展而自行得到纠正，但也有许多语言错误必须得到及时的纠正，这种动态"负面"输入对学生的语言发展极为重要。

4. 第二版教材更加强调语言学习的自主性。语言教学要让学生获得语言知识，但是也要让学生学会自己去发现语言知识。学生通常必须在有意义的思维活动的基础上，在真实性交际需要的驱动下才能寻找到能刺激语言发展的语言形式。第二版教材重新设计了许多符合当代青年学生特点的任务，鼓励他们将自己的生活经验与语言活动以及语言学习联系起来，从而获得自主发现语言形式的机会。

5. 第二版教材增加了大量的任务型活动 (Task-based Activities) 和研究型活动 (Enquiry-based Activities)。有的活动印在学生用书上，有的放在教师用书上。一般来讲，在学生用书中提供的活动要求学生独立思考，锤炼语言；安排在教师用书上的任务在开展活动时由教师复印后发给学生，这更有利于教师组织课堂活动。编写组在实验中发现，语言学习的机会不仅产生于课前已经准备好的活动中，也产生于课堂活动的过程中。

第一册学生用书修改了部分对话和阅读文章；调整了阅读理解题，使之更加简练，概括性更强。原来的"角色表演"改为"任务型"活动，第三部分的扩充阅读后也增加了"任务型"活动。第三部分的词汇学习 (In other words) 作了较大的改动，改动后的训练强调在语境中理解词语的意义和用法的能力，数量上由原来的10个左右的词语改为现在的5个，每个词语的例句印在教师用书上。写作部分 (Writing) 的改动主要在第二项 (b) 上，第二版教材重新设计了大部分练习，使写作的目的更加明确、具体，教师用书上增加了辅助材料，教师可以根据学生的实际情况组织活动，帮助学生完成写作任务。第二版教材中的文化学习 (Cultural Information) 增加了练习，以期提高学生理解英美文化的能力，学会文化对比和文化批评。 这些补充练习都印在教师用书中，教师可根据实际情况决定取舍。

另外，第二版教材的书后配上了多媒体学习课件。该课件是与学生用书配套的学习光盘，是该教材立体化建设的组成部分，但并不是每单元的内容都与学生用书完全一致。该课件供英语专业本科基础阶段使用，旨在培养学生听、说、读、写、译的综合技能。主要通过语言基础训练与篇章讲解分析，使学生提高语篇理解能力，具备口头与书面表达的能力。每单元包括单元目标、情景对话、课文学习、文化点滴和扩展练习。该课件内容完整丰富，编排循序渐进，融语言知识、交际技能和教学技巧于一体。媒体表现形式多样，听说部分配有生动的动画、声音和图片，练习部分具有交互性，并设有阶段测试、答疑、沙龙等功能，可供学生自主性学习使用。此外，第二版的教师用书书后新增了多媒体教学课件，该课件为教师课堂教学提供了丰富的参考内容，并且增加了许多任务型和研究型的训练项目，教师在教学中可根据学生的情况选用。

编者建议教师在教学前仔细阅读教师用书，在掌握基本教学技巧和活动组织技巧的基础上进行发挥和创造。

编写组特别感谢两位美国语言教育和教师培训方面的专家 Randi Steckler 和 Michael Steckler 夫妇， 他们耐心地帮助我们修改书稿， 他们的无私帮助使我们的第二版教材在教学设计和语言质量上都更臻于完善， 教材中若还有谬误， 则是编写组的责任。

编写组抱着认真负责的态度开展修改工作，在修改中尽量考虑到我国英语专业基础阶段外语教学的情况、学生的常用学习策略和广大教师的教学习惯。但是百密一漏，第二版教材中一定还会有许多疏漏，我们恳请广大教师和学生提出宝贵的批评意见。

《综合英语教程》编写组
于华东师范大学
2004年7月

《综合英语教程》为教育部委托编写的普通高等教育 "九五" 国家级重点教材出版项目,是为我国师范院校英语专业学生编写的一本面向二十一世纪的英语专业基础教材,也可供教育学院和社会自学者使用。全书共四册,由学生用书,教师用书和录音磁带组成。

本教材力图反映近年来国内外在应用语言学、心理学和英语教学研究方面的成果。编者认为,基础英语的教材应该处理好基础知识的掌握,能力的培养和文化知识的学习三者之间的关系。

一、基础知识的掌握

基础知识指英语语言基础知识,具体地说,基础阶段的学生应该掌握下列内容:

1. 语言体系知识 (Knowledge of language system)

语言体系知识指语音、词汇和语法结构等方面的内容。基础阶段一般只有两年的时间,要在这么短的时间内完成大纲所规定的语言知识的传授,是一件十分艰巨的工作。这就要求教材提供严密、详细而又完整的训练项目,有效地覆盖和循环各个阶段的语言知识。本书编者力图通过循序渐进的方式,使学生逐步掌握系统的英语语言基础知识,为他们提高语言交际能力打下坚实的基础。

2. 话语知识 (Knowledge of discourse)

教材还必须向学生提供话语知识。语言教学必须努力创造交际气氛,在这种氛围中,学生和教师的语言要带有明确的交际目的。他们不仅用语言进行意义交流,还进行情感交流。唯有这样,语言才能真正发挥交际功能,学生才能真正从心理上感受到语言的力量。这样的语言学习就具有了高度的心理真实性。然而,一切具备这种氛围的语言活动都必须建立在连续的话语基础之上,学生必须学习种种话语交际所要求的知识,譬如,如何开始谈话,如何结束谈话,如何有效地组织信息,如何利用和处理对方的信息,如何掌握使用语言的分寸等等。系统地获取这些知识,不能仅仅依靠教师的讲解,必须以大量的在话语环境下进行的实践活动作保证。本教材的每一个单元都围绕一个话题展开,其目的就是为了给学生营造一个话语环境,使学生能将语言形式和话语情景紧密地结合在一起,以利于学生提高运用语言的"得体程度"(Appropriacy)。

3. "常用语"知识 (Knowledge of formulae)

大量的语言研究证实,语言交际并不完全依靠百分之百的创造性。"流利性"和"准确性" (Native-like fluency and native-like accuracy) 都是有条件的。在交际者谈论熟悉的话题时,语言的流利性和准确性要明显高于谈论陌生的话题。所谓"熟悉",事实上就是满足两个基本条件:(1) 说话者知道要说什么,也就是说,说话者对谈话内容有大体上合适的知识范围;(2) 说话者知道若干谈论此话题和内容所要用到的关键性的词语。这种词语就是谈论该话题的"常用语"(Formulae或Routinized expressions)。研究还证实,一个人在自然的谈话 (Spontaneous conversation) 中,大部分语言是属于"常用语"范畴的。因此,掌握大量英美人日常生活中的常用语,并且懂得何时何地使用它们,是提高流利性和准确性的重要手段。本教材在这方面提供了大量的内容,并且有足够的练习以达到巩固的目的。

二、能力的培养

本书着重培养学生以下几方面的能力：

1. 学习者的学习策略能力 (Learner's strategies)

本教材吸收了近年来心理语言学研究方面的若干成果。编者在关心语言内容的同时，也十分关心学习者学习策略和学习能力的培养。心理学家认为，学习效果与学习者的心理准备状态 (Preparedness) 有着密切的关系，准备状态越好，学习效率就越高。其次，第二语言的习得与语言学习者的语言意识程度 (Language awareness) 有密切的关系，良好的语言意识能促进语言习得。第三，在语言学习中，语言活动的过程比语言活动的结果更为重要。因此如何提高学习者对语言学习的准备程度和对语言形式的意识程度，同时又能将其吸引到参与语言活动中来，这是编者十分关心的问题。为了培养学生正确的学习策略，本教材采用了两种方法：(1) 提高学生有意识的准备程度；(2) 为学生创造"隐性准备"的条件。前者通过大量的自主学习项目来实现，这些活动项目要求学生通过自我发现、独立工作和自由活动来完成 (Self-discovery, autonomous study and uninhibited practice)。而"隐性准备"的条件主要是通过重复话题来创造。教材中的每一个单元为一个话题，每一个话题虽然在本册中只出现一次，但在全套教材中反复出现。编者通过控制语言练习的项目和难度，使得前面的单元成为后续单元的"隐性准备"，而后续单元又成为前面单元的复习。

2. 语言尝试能力 (The ability to experiment with language)

"语言冒险" (Linguistic adventure) 精神与语言发展速度有着直接的关系。为学生创造"语言冒险"的机会是一本好教材必须具备的条件。学生的这种能力并不是自动产生的，而是需要语言教师的培养和教材提供机会。因此编者在设计语言练习时，充分考虑到学生所关心的话题，设计了大量的学生可以自由发挥的训练项目，为他们思想的飞翔开辟广阔的空间。

3. 语言思维能力 (Higher-order thinking ability)

语言学习的最高境界是学习者能完全用目标语进行符合交际要求的思维活动。但是我们的外语教学长期以来重视记忆、背诵，忽视语言学习过程中所发生的认知活动。没有思想的语言是无用的语言，长久依赖背诵而获得的语言是苍白空洞的，用这种方法培养出来的人必定是"流利准确"的废话制造者 (Fluent fool)。同时，近年来的一些研究报告也认为，语言活动与认知活动的结合是获得语言交际能力的必经之路。因此，本教材的编者在编写过程中，十分重视那些有助于开拓学生认知能力，促进思维能力发展的语言训练项目。

4. 语言教师的职业能力 (Professionalism)

由于《综合英语教程》是我国师范类院校的教材，我们是在为未来培养教师，因而如何把职业特点体现在语言学习中也是我们重点考虑的一个问题。我们通过大量的与师范职业有关的语言活动，使学生在学习语言的同时能够接受初步的职业训练。因此，书中的许多练习既有语言训练的价值，又有职业训练的作用。

三、文化知识的学习

语言是文化的载体，文化又是语言的土壤。现代语言学认为，无论语言理解 (Understanding) 还是语言使用 (Production) 都必须依赖使用语言的人所具有的社会、文化和语言等方面的知识。语言使用者在语言活动中，不断地将其自身的社会经历、文化背景和文化知识作为其思维活动的重要依据。缺乏这些知识，语言理解就会变得异常困难或是错误百出。倘若学生在初级阶段尚能应付过关，而他们在中级和高级阶段的学习将难以为继。文化学习的另一个特殊意义是可以使人开阔视野，避免采用母语文化的框架去阐释异邦文化，从而加深文化间的隔阂。因而，本教材的编者认为，学生在学习英语的同时，必须高度重视英语国家的社会文化知识。在这方面，本教材做了大量的工作，每一单元之后列出了英语国家的文化背景专栏，使学生能够接受到比较系统的文化知识的熏陶。

本书是《综合英语教程》学习用书第一册，全书共15个单元，每单元由三大部分组成：听说训练 (Listening and Speaking Activities)、阅读理解和语言操练 (Reading Comprehension and Language Activities) 以及扩展性练习 (Extended Activities)。

在第一部分听说训练中，每单元教一至两个常用的交际功能，以对话的形式介绍给学生。学生的口语练习，从有控制的对话开始，逐步过渡到半开放性的训练。最后，学生要能够在预定的场合中，得体地表达这种语言功能。该部分还提供了大量的口语常用句型 (Formulae)，熟练掌握和正确理解其交际含义，可以使学生较快地学会说地道的英语口语。第一部分还附有一些较为高级的口语表达方式，可供学有余力的学生选学。

第二部分围绕课文阅读以及课文中所涉及的语言重点和难点，展开全面的语言交际活动。目的是通过不同的交际方式，使学生能够深刻地理解课文，掌握规定的若干词语和句型用法，并能简明扼要地复述课文大意。在复述课文时，本册为学生提供了语言和内容两方面的提示。课文中的语言重点和难点通过随后的书面练习进行训练。

第三部分为扩展性练习。针对第一和第二部分的教学重点，该部分提供了听写、阅读、语法、惯用法、翻译和写作等训练项目，其目的是巩固已学到的知识，同时开阔学生的视野。写作练习分别由有控制的练习与自由写作两部分组成。有控制的练习要求学生练习单句，如句子的扩展、简单回答问题和评论；自由写作要求学生根据课文填写表格、改写、仿写段落等等。建议教师批改有控制的写作部分，并定期与学生交流。自由写作部分，教师可以只检查，不批改，以此为学生营造一个较为宽松的写作练习气氛。

为了满足师范教育的特殊要求，本书试图在语言训练活动中融入教学技能训练。编者将若干重要的教学技能穿插到各单元的语言活动之中。如"教学演讲"(Presentation) 体现在各课课文复述和讨论中；"课堂英语"(Classroom English) 体现在"练习指令"(Exercise Instructions) 中。

考虑到我们今天的学生是明天的教师，所以他们语音基础功十分重要。为此，本册专门设计了点面结合的语音训练练习。点的训练体现在第一册书后所附的四课语音集中训练中，它们基础上覆盖了基础英语阶段的语音要求，面的训练体现在各课的语音练习中，使学生有机会在细水长流式的练习中逐步纠正各种语音顽症。但是由于各地学生方言和中学教学状况的差异，教师在教学时可根据实际情况决定取舍。

本册的教学进度，编者建议每周1单元，每单元6课时。

本教材的前期编写工作共有十多位人员参与，其中有华东师范大学外语系的朱钟毅教授、张春柏教授，戴天佑副教授、王世静副教授以及镇江师专的贾德霖教授和原山西师专的白世俊副教授。安徽六安师专、广西柳州师专、河南新乡师专、佳木斯大学师范学院，福建南平师专、四川成都师专、广东韶关大学外语系、山东菏泽师专、河北廊坊师专、湖北黄冈师范学院、漳州师范学院、浙江湖州师专 (排名不分先后) 承担了本教材的试用工作，他们为本书贡献了不少宝贵的意见和建议。上海外国语大学的李观仪教授和美国圣奥洛夫大学 (St. Olaf College) 的 Richard C. Buckstead 教授在本教材的设计和成书过程中给予了不少指点和帮助。我们在此向他们表示诚挚的感谢。

复旦大学孙骊教授 (主审)、教育部高等学校外语专业教学指导委员会委员华南理工大学秦秀白教授 (主审)、教育部高等学校外语专业教学指导委员会委员北京师范大学王蔷教授、北京师范大学武尊民教授、湖北黄冈师范学院蓝葆春教授和河南新乡师专郭爱先副教授审阅了本书，在此深表谢意。编者同时欢迎读者提出宝贵的意见和批评。

编　者
1998年5月
于华东师范大学

Units	Titles	Functions and Communication
1	The Snake Bite	<li> Expressing feelings of distress or annoyance <li> Talking about a character in a literary account <li> Appreciating literary works such as fables and poems in related topics
2	He Was My Father	<li> Talking about what was im/possible when discussing childhood life <li> Talking about cultural differences in childhood education <li> Critiquing Chinese cultural practice of childhood education <li> Describing a person
3	Understanding Your Owner	<li> Expressing disapproval and dissatisfaction <li> Discussing pet-keeping, and the issues of mutual understanding <li> Fairy tales in English speaking cultures
4	Water Cycle	<li> Expressing different degrees of certainties <li> Talking about wastewater treatment and environmental protection <li> Science / technology / resources' impact on environment
5	Is My Team Ploughing	<li> Asking and answering questions <li> Giving opinions and impressions <li> Talking about issues of life such as work, play, friend and love

Contents

Contents

Contents

Unit 1

The Snake Bite

Introduction

In this unit, you will learn to use English for

- Expressing feelings of distress or annoyance
- Talking about a character in a literary account
- Appreciating literary works such as fables and poems in related topics

PART 1 Communicative Activities

1 ▶ Interactive listening and speaking
A Listening

🎧 In this recording, a father is telling how he and his daughters felt about a chicken farm

they visited. Before you listen, predict how they would feel?

The father and his daughters would feel _____ about the chickens and the farm they visited.

Ecstatic	Upset	Distressful	Relaxed
Disgusted	Excited	Annoyed	Angry
Fearful	Amazed	Frightened	Shocked

Now, listen and check your predictions.

B Talk

1. What actually sickened the father and his daughters on the chicken farm?
2. Can you describe what they saw on the farm?
3. Do you agree that the chicken farm industry is a disgrace?

Talk about your feelings

The father said that "it sickened him to see how chickens were raised in the cage". For a milder degree of unpleasant / distressing experience, people may as well say "it bugs me to see how chickens were treated on the farm". Now, talk about what sickens you and what bugs you in your life. And then write your feelings on the lines below.

It sickens me to see / It sickens me that …	*It bugs me to see / It bugs me that …*
(1) _____	(4) _____
(2) _____	(5) _____
(3) _____	(6) _____

2 ▶ **Story time**

Work out a short story in pairs based on the following picture. You may tell the story from the first person perspective (acting the role of the little girl in the picture) or the third person perspective (as a viewer of the cartoon).

3 > What are they for?

There are many ways of expressing distress and annoyance. Read the following and match the functions with the actual words spoken.

Actual words spoken	Functions
a. I just can't remember that girl's name, it's really bugging me.	1. Your work is delayed by someone. Say to him / her that you are annoyed.
b. Why on earth didn't you tell me the truth?	2. Children keep asking you to take them to the beach. But you don't want to go. Ask them to stop bothering you.
c. You kept me waiting for over an hour. What have you been busy with?	
d. I can't say I'm at all pleased about your delay.	3. You feel annoyed because you cannot remember the girl's name.
e. I wish you'd stop pestering me. We're not going to the beach and that's final.	4. You are annoyed by one of your classmates because you dislike his bragging.
f. I'm most unhappy at his bragging.	5. You've become impatient for having to wait for an hour.
	6. You lost your temper because someone had kept you in the dark.

4 > More sentences

Read the following sentences that are frequently used and complete the matching exercise.

1. It really annoys me that she never returns the books she borrows.

2. It galled him bitterly that his father gambled again.

3. She never stopped complaining while we were on vacation. It really got on my nerves.

4. Turn that music down — it's driving me mad.

5. What really gets under my skin is people who talk while I'm trying to concentrate on my work.

6. Having to stay in and work on a sunny day like this is a real drag.

7. My tape recorder's broken down again. It's a nuisance, isn't it?

8. We'd be OK if we could get this stupid gate to open properly.

Matching Exercise

Put the above sentence number into a suitable blank.

a. You feel bored because you have to work and cannot enjoy yourself on a sunny day. _____

b. You cannot open the gate and you become very annoyed and impatient. _____

c. You are annoyed by her continual complaints during your holiday. _____

d. You feel a little angry because a woman does not return the books she has borrowed. _____

e. He was upset because his father gambled again. _____

f. You cannot stand the loud music any more. Express your annoyance. _____

g. Say that you don't like people talking while you are at work. _____

h. You feel distressed because your tape recorder has failed to work again. _____

● Proverb

If we are bound to forgive an enemy, we are not bound to trust him.

PART **2** Reading and Language Activities

Text   The Snake Bite

▶ Pre-reading tasks   **Complete the following tasks.**

1) What are the specific names for these melons?

2) What should we do to rescue someone that was bitten by a poisonous snake? List at least three things that we can do to save his life:

(a) _____

(b) _____

(c) _____

> Read the story, and list the things that had been done to save the boy's life.

In the West Bottom we raised watermelons and muskmelons for the market, but the house melon-and-garden patch was back of the barn on the edge of the cane field. One day I took a corn knife from the tool shed and went out to get me a watermelon for my own use. I was forbidden to carry a corn knife, which had a blade longer than my arm. But it was the best thing there was for cutting a melon. One swipe and your melon was in two.

I was going along thumping melons for a ripe one when all at once my foot seemed to come down on something like a needle. I thought I had stepped into a mess of sandburs.

But when I looked, there was a rattler. I knew all about rattlers never being supposed to strike without warning. And I knew the sound of a rattler as well as I knew the notes of a quail. It was figured later that maybe this one didn't have time to rattle. I must have stepped right into his mouth. I lit out for the house, yelling. I was sure I was going to die. That was all I could think of.

Mamma whipped off her apron and tied the strings around my leg above the knee. She made me lie on the sofa in the front room and put Martha to watch me. There was not a man on the place or a horse in the lot. The nearest habitation was Mr. Howell's, but he had no horse. The next nearest was Jim Anderson's, exactly half a mile away by the shortcut through a field. Mamma made for the Andersons. One of the Anderson boys jumped on a horse and started for town. A son of Clark who worked for the Andersons, drove Mamma home. When she got there, she found that Martha had taken off the apron strings because I had cried that they were too tight. Mamma put them back, yanking them so tight that I screamed.

Then Mamma went to the porch to watch the road from town. Following the line between the Anderson and the Howell claims, the road ran along the crest of a rise so that you got the silhouette of anything that passed over it. I could always pick out our buggy and Tom, especially with papa driving. Anxious to get his nose in the manger, Tom would break into a gallop if you would let him, and papa always did.

Herb Anderson's instructions had been first to find Papa. If he couldn't do that right away, to find Dr. McKenzie. If he couldn't find him, to find Dr. Field or some other doctor.

Mamma was watching to see whose rig would show up. Every now and then she would come inside and try to get me to stop yelling.

At length she said "It's your father."

Comprehension work

A Emergency

List the things that had been done as an emergency response to the snake bite, and comment if they are correct. And why? The first one has been done as an example.

No.	Things that happened?	Correct?	Why do you think so?
1	The boy lit for the house, yelling.	Probably not.	Running and yelling put him in danger because they would speed up blood circulation. He should quickly squeeze the poisonous liquid out of the wound, or try to stop blood circulation around the wound.
2			
3			
4			
5			
6			
7			
8			

B Saved!

The story did not tell us how the father saved the boy's life. Work in small groups to continue the story by designing a new ending.

Now, write your ending in about 100 words after the discussion.

C Poem reading.

Read the poem *Snake* by Emily Dickinson and complete the task of Poem analysis.

Poem	Poem analysis
Snake *By Emily Dickinson* A narrow Fellow in the Grass Occasionally rides — You may have met Him — did you not His notice sudden is — The Grass divides as with a Comb — A spotted shaft is seen — And then it closes at your feet And opens further on — He likes a Boggy Acre A Floor too cool for Corn — Yet when a Boy, and Barefoot — I more than once at Noon Have passed, I thought, a Whip lash Unbraiding in the Sun When stooping to secure it It wrinkled, and was gone — Several of nature's People I know, and they know me — I feel for them a transport Of cordiality — But never met this Fellow Attended, or alone Without a tighter breathing And Zero at the Bone —	The poet speaker did not use the word snake in the whole poem. But we can feel its presence throughout the poem. 1. Look at the physical shape of the poem, what feature does it have? 2. Which stanzas describe the physical features of a snake? 3. Which stanzas describe the poet speaker's feelings and emotions at this infamous creature?

Discuss these questions about the poem.

Stanza 1

- What is special about *a narrow Fellow*?
- What is special about *rides*?
- What should the full sentence be for *his notice sudden is*?

Stanza 2

- What do the words *divides*, *closes*, and *opens* describe?

● What kind of physical feature does the snake have?

Stanzas 3 – 4

● What kind of place does the snake like to stay at?

● What happened when the barefooted poet speaker met the snake?

Stanzas 5 – 6

● *Feel ... a transport of cordiality*: what kind of feeling is it? And whom is this feeling toward?

● But what about his feeling towards a snake?

2 ▷ Language work

A Fill out the following blanks with words or phrases from the text.

1. _____ _____ _____ the little girl caught sight of a rattler and _____ in fear.

2. It is _____ that the boy can get home in three minutes _____ _____ _____ through a supermarket.

3. The corporation has run into trouble and it _____ to be _____ _____ _____ _____ bankruptcy.

4. The parking _____ is _____ _____ the office building.

5. There is no air on Mars, so _____ is impossible on the planet.

6. In some cities people are _____ to _____ small animals, because pets may spread diseases and create health problems.

7. We waited at the bus stop for twenty minutes. _____ _____, the bus _____ _____ in the distance.

B Rewrite the following sentences with the expressions in the box.

the crest	make for	strike	show up
pick out	light out (for)	break into a gallop	must have done

1. When it was disturbed, the deer rushed away and disappeared in the forest.

   _____

2. All the passengers rushed out of the waiting hall to a safe place when the fire broke out.

   _____

3. Tommy promised to come over, but he has not appeared yet.

   _____

4. The light was on in the office for the whole night. It must be that somebody had forgotten to turn it off.

   _____

5. The escaped prisoner hoped that no one could recognise him in the crowd.

   _____

6. When the movie was over, the audience moved towards the exits.

_____

7. The wolves approached the sheep ready to attack.

_____

8. After a short rest, the army climbed over the top of the mountain.

_____

C Word study.

　a. **Give the meanings of the following words or expressions used in the text. You may use an English-English Dictionary. Then give a sentence to illustrate their meanings and usage.**

　　1. on the edge of

_____

　　2. for one's own use

_____

　　3. shortcut

_____

　　4. every now and then

_____

　　5. at length

_____

　b. **Each of the following clues has an example sentence. Use the prompts to produce other sentences with the same pattern as the example.**

　　1. Prompt: house melon-and-garden patch / back / barn / on the edge of
　　　　Example: The house melon-and-garden patch was back of the barn on the edge of the cane field.
　　　　a. they / live / cottage / on the edge of
　　　　b. villa / stand / on the edge of / orchard
　　　　c. tree / on the edge of / cliff
　　2. Prompt: I / get / watermelon / for my own use
　　　　Example: I went out to get a watermelon for my own use.
　　　　a. he / buy / electric shaver / for his own use
　　　　b. we / bring / camera / for our own use
　　　　c. mayor / build / villa / for his own use
　　3. Prompt: nearest / Jim Anderson's / half a mile / by the shortcut
　　　　Example: The next nearest was Jim Anderson's, exactly half a mile away by the shortcut through a field.
　　　　a. dining-hall / twenty meters / by the shortcut
　　　　b. nearest hospital / No. 1 People's hospital / 200 meters / by the shortcut

    c. take / you / 5 minutes / cinema / by the shortcut

4. Prompt: every now and then / she / come / try to

   Example: Every now and then she would come inside and try to get me to stop yelling.

    a. dog / jump up / every now and then / while I'm

    b. every now and then / robber / look out of the windows / while his partners

    c. every now and then / student / doze off

5. Prompt: at length / she / say

   Example: At length she said "It's your father".

    a. at length / girl / find out / key

    b. at length / we / finish / entrance examination / begin / vacation

    c. at length / family / say goodbye / old / refrigerator / new

PART 3 Extended Activities

1 Dictation

2 Read more

Read the following story. Work with your partner to put the pictures in a correct order. Then match the pictures with the subtitles.

Misunderstand

    This is an old story. It dates back, indeed, to the year of 1864, when the pet of a British regiment, stationed in Jamaica, was a baboon. He was a meditative and extremely thoughtful baboon, and his habits and manners provided continual amusement for the officers, before whose mess-room windows his dwelling was placed. He was on a long, light chain, but even with this restraint he managed to get into a good deal of mischief. As, for instance, on one day, when he thought himself insulted by a certain young officer, and instantly fell to beating the mess-room windows with such terrific effect that his habitation was removed to a less commanding spot. Here his amusements still went on, however. Any living creature that ventured within his chain-radius was apt to have a busy minute or two, and the unhappy fowls, who often strayed within reach, were grabbed instantly, and sometimes strangled, though he more often amused himself by plucking or half-plucking his unhappy prisoner before releasing it.

One fowl, however, he took a sudden and violent fancy for. He grabbed it, it is true, but he neither plucked it nor wrung its neck, but, instead, fondled it with such demonstrative affection that quite possibly the unfortunate cock would have preferred plucking. He squeezed it, he stroked it, rubbed it, nursed it, held it aloft and danced it, released it for a moment, and playfully hauled it back by the leg when it made for liberty. The bird did not in any way return his affection; in fact, altogether misunderstood it. But the baboon persevered, and held firmly on to his pet. He felt confident of winning it over by persistent kindness, and since his earlier demonstrations had proved unsuccessful, he renewed them with more vigor. He stroked it the other way, rubbed it more persistently, danced it more quickly, and squeezed it a good deal harder. But even these attentions failed to rouse its affection, and at last, in the midst of an extra-friendly hug, the cock died, misunderstanding the devoted baboon to the last.

He was overcome with grief. To think that at last, when he had found himself a creature he could really love, it should die before he could obtain the return of his affection. It was very sad. He set about the last sad rites with every manifestation of sorrow. In solemn grief

Notes

1. regiment: a unit of the army
2. Jamaica: a member country of the Commonwealth in the Caribbean Sea (牙买加)
3. baboon: a large monkey (狒狒)
4. meditative: sentimental, thinking deeply (the word here is used ironically)
5. mess-room: (military) a dining room
6. dwelling: living place
7. instantly fell to beating ... : began beating ... right away
8. a less commanding spot: a less important place where the baboon would not be likely to arouse a great deal of interest from the soldiers
9. have a busy minute or two: be quick to get away from the baboon (understatement)
10. strayed within reach: happened to get within the reach of the baboon
11. plucking: pulling out feathers
12. fondle: caress, touch tenderly
13. made for liberty: tried to escape
14. misunderstanding the devoted baboon to the last: not being able to understand why the baboon treated him like this even to the last minute of his life
15. He was overcome with grief: He was very sad, too sad to know what to do
16. last rites: ceremonies for the dead
17. fortnight: two weeks

he buried his departed playmate at the foot of a tall tree, where the grass might grow and the birds sing over its grave. Then he sat down before the grave and mourned; neglected all his usual amusements and mourned sorely day by day for a fortnight. But at the end of that time he could bear his grief no longer; so he dug up his departed pet and ate it!

A The subtitles.

1. Though chained, the baboon managed to pluck or half-pluck any fowls within his reach.
2. He took a sudden and violent fancy for one fowl and showed demonstrative affection for it.
3. He held it aloft.
4. He playfully hauled it back by the leg when the fowl made for liberty.
5. He felt confident of winning it over by persistent kindness.
6. In the midst of an extra-friendly hug, the cock died, misunderstanding the lover to the last.
7. In solemn grief he buried his departed playmate at the foot of a tall tree, where the grass might grow and the birds sing over its grave.
8. He could bear his grief no longer; so he dug up his departed pet and ate it.

B True / False / Not Mentioned (NM).

1. The baboon who was the pet of a British regiment lived with the soldiers in their house.
2. The baboon preferred thinking to mischief-making.
3. When the baboon was insulted, he was not likely to take his revenge on the enemy.
4. One of the baboon's amusements was to grab any living creature that was within his reach.
5. The baboon usually killed his unhappy captives by plucking or half-plucking their feathers.
6. He liked one fowl he had caught, but the fowl could not stand his fondling.
7. This was the first fowl the baboon had ever eaten.
8. The story is a vivid illustration of the importance of communication.

C Activity

An encounter in heaven

Suppose the baboon died of grief over the death of the cock. The two souls met in heaven finally where they could communicate with each other in a common language. Design a scene of their encounter and the conversation between them.

3 Grammar work

Correct the mistakes in the following sentences.

1. The mother forbade her children eating sweets because she didn't want their teeth to be ruined.
2. The manager managed to solve the problem, but at length, he failed.
3. Richard and Janet decided amuse themselves by playing computer games.
4. The teacher found some students to lose interest in literature.
5. In some countries, war forces many people leave their native places.
6. The little boy made the dog to obey his order.
7. The police watched two burglars to break into a house.
8. Mr. Jackson persuaded his son to stay on the farm, but the boy didn't listen to him.
9. The manager let the secretary to mail the letter.

4 Word formation

Fill out the following blanks with derivatives of the words in the brackets.

1. The government is trying to control population _____ (grow).
2. If it's a choice between high pay and job _____ (secure), I'd prefer to keep my job.
3. I haven't got a ruler with me. Can you tell me the _____ (wide), _____ (long) and _____ (high) of the box?
4. Because of the _____ (cold) of the weather, we stayed indoors, dreaming of the _____ (warm) of summer.
5. I don't mind _____ (untidy) — it's _____ (dirty) that I can't stand.

13

6. I played the piano just for my own _____ (amuse).

7. Our _____ (depart) was delayed because of bad weather.

8. I was struck by her _____ (thoughtful).

> *-ment*, *-ness*, and *-th* are all noun suffixes.
>
> *-ment* is added to a verb to mean a result state of a verb, e.g., develop – development, govern – government.
>
> *-ness* is added to an adjective to form a noun that shows the quality, state or character of the adjective, e.g., dry – dryness, silly – silliness.
>
> *-th* is added to a few verbs and adjectives to form nouns, e.g., grow – growth , wide – width.

 Vocabulary work

Cries of animals

Special verbs refer to the cry, call, or voice of many animals. The following are some examples. Match them appropriately.

dog	quack
cat	howl
duck	bark
pig	grunt
hen	mew
wolf	moo
horse	neigh
cow	cackle

 Translation

Put the following sentences into English.

1. 天开始下雨，她走向附近的一个避雨处。**make for**

2. 她挑了一顶帽子，正好配她的衣服。**pick out**

3. 我等了一个小时，可还是没见他的人影。**show up**

4. 他们觉得还是呆在原地好。**figure**

5. 小岛上发生的地震，造成了23人死亡。**strike**

6. 在离开村子20年后，他终于回到了家。**at length**

7. 她的许多同事已经失去了工作，她总算保住了。**hold on to**

7 Writing

A Work on your own.

Look at the eight pictures in Read more. Write a short explanation or description for each of them in your own words.

1. _____
2. _____
3. _____
4. _____
5. _____
6. _____
7. _____
8. _____

B Never again!

In order to prevent snakebites in future, the villagers have decided to put up a notice near the watermelon patch. Write the notice on their behalf. The notice should first give a brief account of the recent incident of a rattler's strike and then warn the villagers to take precautionary measures if they want to get into the field (in about 150 words).

Watch out for Rattlesnakes!

C ultural Information

Read the passage below, and then complete the task of cultural study.

Friends or Enemies

As in many other cultures, the British and Americans have formed some fixed conceptions about animals. They believe that some animals have their typical features. Here are a few of the examples:

ass	stupid	**monkey**	clever, enjoying playing tricks, but
dog	faithful		not very intelligent or important

15

cat	deceptive	**sheep**	silly, easily controlled and following others without thinking
goose	foolish		
dove	peaceful	**pigeon**	cowardly
bear	ill-tempered		
camel	submissive		
snake	treachery, secretive		
fox	cunning, sexy		
donkey	hard-working		

Cultural Study Task

What cultural conceptions do the Chinese associate with those animals? Ask the people around you for their ideas about the animals.

He Was My Father

Introduction

In this unit, you will learn to use English for

▶ Talking about what was im/possible when discussing childhood life
▶ Talking about cultural differences in childhood education
▶ Critiquing Chinese cultural practice of childhood education
▶ Describing a person

PART 1 Communicative Activities

1 ▶ Interactive listening and speaking

A Listening

In this recording, two friends (Mary and Helen) are talking about life of childhood. Listen, and choose the correct answers from the choices. (There may be more than one choice for each question.)

1. What does Mary think of one's childhood?
   a. It is the most important period in one's life.
   b. It is the happiest period in one's life.
   c. It is the most important, but may not be the happiest period in one's life.
2. What does Helen think of one's childhood?
   a. She agrees with Mary.
   b. She sounds like in disagreement with Mary.
   c. She sounds like having no opinions of her own.
3. Judging by the way of talking between the two friends, what kind of personality do you think each of them has?
   a. Both of them are opinionated people.
   b. Mary is an opinionated person, but Helen is not.
   c. Helen is an opinionated person, but Mary is not.
4. Mary does not think that children are very happy, because _____.
   a. they are not allowed to have their own ideas
   b. they are under a lot of pressure to achieve what their parents expect of them
   c. they are not allowed to do what they want to
5. What's Helen's opinion about adult's life?
   a. It's more tiring and unpleasant.
   b. It's carefree and independent.
   c. Adults can enjoy freedom.
6. According to Mary, who might be responsible for unhappiness of many children?
   a. Strict teachers.
   b. Demanding parents.
   c. Permissive parents.

B Debating

A Tiger Mother's Parenting

Recently a book entitled *The Battle Hymn of a Tiger Mother* ignites a wide range of heated conversations over what is counted as good parenting in both China and US. The author, Amy Chua, is a Chinese-American professor from the Law School at Yale University. She is well-known for strict parenting principles for her two daughters. Below in the table is a list of her rules for her two daughters, and her arguments. Matt Comynes, an expert on China, has been working in China over ten years. On the right side is a list of his comments. Which side do you support? Why?

Amy's rules for her two daughters
1. They are not allowed to attend sleepover.
2. They are not allowed to learn any other musical instruments except for violin or piano, and play only classic music.

3. They are not allowed to have playdate.
4. They are not allowed to watch TV or play computer games.
5. They must achieve A for every course they take. They should not have any excuses for whatever, just get the job done.
6. They should overcome all issues on their own.

Amy's argument	Matt's comment
• High expectation produces more self-esteem in children if it is coupled with love and parental commitment. • Children grow up quickly under push and pressure. • Children have greater potentials than parents believe in themselves. They are capable of doing more than what we believe that they are able to. • Nothing is fun until you're good at it. • You can achieve what you want if you work hard at it. It just needs practice and hard work. Once you get over the hurdle, it's easy and fun, and you will enjoy doing it. • My way is not new, deeply rooted in Chinese culture, and also in American culture, for example, those teachings by Benjamin Franklin.	• Discipline and hard work can help a bit no matter how smart you're. But they have limitations. • This parenting practice may be good for training work ethic. • The downside is lack of creativity or innovation in children. • This parenting is good for the children in China right now, but looking forward, maybe we need more diverse ways of education.

Notes

1. Sleepover: A sleepover, also known as a pajama party or a slumber party, is a party most commonly held by children or teenagers, where a guest or guests are invited to stay overnight at the home of a friend.

2. Playdate: A play date or playdate is an arranged appointment for children to get together for a few hours to play. Playdates have become the standard for children of many western cultures because the work schedules for busy parents, along with media warnings about leaving children unattended, prevent the kind of play that children of other generations participated in.

C Group Discussion.

Benjamin Franklin and His Thirteen Virtues

Amy argues that her practice is actually both Chinese and American in nature. Work in small groups to study the Benjamin Franklin's thirteen virtues listed below. Which of the virtues are both Chinese and American? Would you like to develop them? Give your reasons.

Thirteen Virtues

Franklin sought to cultivate his character by a plan of thirteen virtues, which he developed at age 20 (in 1726) and continued to practice in some form for the rest of his life. His autobiography lists his thirteen virtues as:

"Temperance. Eat not to dullness; drink not to elevation."

"Silence. Speak not but what may benefit others or yourself; avoid trifling conversation."

"Order. Let all your things have their places; let each part of your business have its time."

"Resolution. Resolve to perform what you ought; perform without fail what you resolve."

"Frugality. Make no expense but to do good to others or yourself; i.e., waste nothing."

"Industry. Lose no time; be always employed in something useful; cut off all unnecessary actions."

"Sincerity. Use no hurtful deceit; think innocently and justly, and, if you speak, speak accordingly."

"Justice. Wrong none by doing injuries, or omitting the benefits that are your duty."

"Moderation. Avoid extremes; forbear resenting injuries so much as you think they deserve."

"Cleanliness. Tolerate no uncleanliness in body, clothes, or habitation."

"Tranquility. Be not disturbed at trifles, or at accidents common or unavoidable."

"Chastity. Rarely use venery but for health or offspring, never to dullness, weakness, or the injury of your own or another's peace or reputation."

"Humility. Imitate Jesus and Socrates."

 2 ▶ **What are they for?**

There are many ways of expressing possibility and impossibility. Read the following and match the functions with the actual words spoken.

Actual words spoken	Functions
a. The job can be done by Wednesday if I get extra help.	1. Say to your friends that they may be able to make some money if they invest well.

b. Take your umbrella — you might need it.

c. There's a possibility that she'll lose her job.

d. Unfortunately, the manager is very busy so it will be impossible for him to see you today.

e. Alice can't be at home. I saw her just now in the cafe.

f. It's still possible to make some money if you invest wisely.

2. Say it is possible for you to finish the work by Wednesday if you get some help.

3. Say it is impossible that Alice is at home, for you saw her in the cafe a moment ago.

4. Ask your father to take his umbrella because you think it may rain today.

5. You think it possible that the woman will lose her job.

6. You tell the visitor that the manager cannot possibly see him today.

3 More sentences

Read the following sentences that are frequently used and complete the matching exercise.

1. I'm not sure why I couldn't fall asleep. Perhaps it was the coffee.

2. They have a room of their own — possibly for the first time in their lives.

3. He didn't want to admit that this could be the end of his marriage.

4. There's just a chance that she may have left her keys in the office, so I'm going to have a look.

5. Try it! You never know, you might be lucky.

6. There's no way you're going to get the job without good references.

7. Sending Sandra a letter was out of the question, because her husband might intercept it.

8. "Please let me go to the party," Jane begged her mother, but she knew it was hopeless.

Matching Exercise

Put the above sentence number into a suitable blank.

a. It was likely that this would end his marriage, but he didn't want to admit it. _____

b. You couldn't sleep, and you thought maybe it was because of the coffee. _____

c. You encourage your friend to try something because you think he might succeed. _____

d. You thought it was completely impossible for Sandra to receive the letter because her husband would not let her have it. _____

e. You strongly believe that it is impossible for people to get the job if they have not good references. _____

f. You guess it is the first time in their lives to live in their own room. _____

g. Jane begged her mother to let her go to the party, but she knew it was impossible. _____

h. You think it unlikely but still possible that she may have left her keys in the office, so you decide to go and have a look. _____

Proverb

One father is more than a hundred schoolmasters.

PART 2 Reading and Language Activities

Text He Was My Father

▸ Pre-reading tasks **Discuss the following question.**

What makes a man a good father in your opinion?

▸ Read the text

I remember the smell of the soap as he scrubbed his hands. Pungent, because this was for removing ground-in dirt and oil from beneath hardened fingernails and from calloused hands. I can still see the darkness of the water in the basin after he had cleaned his face.

He always spoke to me as he washed before eating his dinner, told me tales of his own childhood and let little drops of moral tuition fall into my lap. "A promise is a promise," he'd say. It was. He never broke one. He was my father.

He drove a London taxi for 40 years. It was a job that paid a decent wage if a man was willing to work 12-hour a day, six days a week.

When I was small, he would sometimes pick up people who were hailing cabs along the way. He wasn't supposed to, not with me in the vehicle. But I was six or seven and was barely noticed.

I could never understand why the passengers treated him with such patronizing disregard. He was "cabbie" and "driver" and "you!" No, he wasn't. He was my dad.

He always looked so strong, so able to protect me, so powerful. Powerful enough to cry when he felt the need. He wept when my grandmother died. Confusing. He came into my room, saw the fear and apprehension on my face, and recited a short prayer with me for my grandma and his mother. He kissed me, held my hand and then drove me to school before putting his 12 hours in. He was my father.

I remember his euphoria when I went to university, the first in his family to do so. Of course he was gauche when I graduated, took too many photographs, and didn't understand the Latin that was spoken before the ceremonial meal. So what? All that concerned this working man in a suit was that his son would not follow in his footsteps. "Do you know why I work such long hours?" he'd ask me. "So that you won't have to."

He couldn't afford to go on holidays with us like other dads. There just wasn't the money. He'd stay on his own, work even longer hours, and live on sandwiches and tea. We'd ring him from a cold beach hotel and tell him how much we missed him. But he knew that. He was my father.

And when my first child was born, this extraordinary ordinary man said very little. Just stared at the baby and then at me. He spoke through his eyes, and I understood. Son, he was telling me, let him be able to say just one thing when he grows up: he was my father.

 Comprehension work

A Work in small groups to complete the following task.

What kind of person is the narrator's father? Use adjectives to describe him. For each adjective you use, find fact from the story.

Adjectives you may use	Details you may find from the story:
As a driver, he is _____ _____ _____	
As a father, he is _____ _____ _____	
As a husband, he is _____ _____ _____	

You may select words from the following lists.

- Serious, professional, conscientious, hardworking, devoted
- Caring, loving, gentle, kind, thoughtful, considerate, faithful, loyal, generous

- Reliable, careful, trustworthy, cooperative
- Straightforward, frank, articulate, aggressive, ambitious
- Secretive, quiet
- Frivolous, changeable, precarious, mean, stingy

B Activity

Select one student to be a celebrity. And design three following questions to interview him / her. The first one has been given as an example.

Interview questions

1) Mr. / Miss XXXX, what kind of person would you select to be your girlfriend / boyfriend?

2) _____

3) _____

4) _____

Now, write a brief report on the results of the interview for your school newspaper in English.

2 Language work

A Idioms

Look up the following idioms in an English-English dictionary, and write their meanings on the lines.

1. fall into one's lap: _____

2. a promise is a promise: _____

3. a stitch in time saves nine: _____

4. one father is more than a hundred schoolmasters: _____

5. follow in one's footsteps: _____

B Word study.

Grind or Ground

Discuss the meaning of **grind** in English and try to make example sentences to illustrate how the verb is used in the structure or context below. Then explain the meaning of the given examples.

v + n

- coffee, wheat, soybeans, rice, meat, cigarette butt
- knifes, teeth, lenses

These things in relation to **grind** are very unpleasant.

People hate **grinding** poverty, **grinding** relationship, **grinding** trouble, or **grinding** noise.

Set phrases

- grindstone, grind one's teeth, grind to a halt
- grind A in / to B

n + v + adv (on, out, against)

- Negotiation grinds on.
- The traffic grinds to a halt when the vehicles approached the site of the accident.
- Coins grind against each other in my bag.

Read the three choices and select the best one to match the phrases or complete the sentences.

1. ground-in dirt
    a. dirt which is ground in the fingernails
    b. dirt which is grounded in the fingernails
    c. dirt which is grinded in the fingernails
2. The meat ball is made of small pieces of beef called _____ in American English, but mince in British English.
    a. grinded beef
    b. ground beef
    c. grounded beef
3. A knife can be made sharper if you _____ on a sandstone.
    a. ground it
    b. grind it
    c. grounded it
4. If something grinds to a halt, it stops _____.
    a. gradually
    b. abruptly
    c. softly
5. Do you _____ your teeth in sleep?
    a. ground
    b. grind
    c. grounded

C Each of the following clues has an example sentence. Use the prompts to produce other sentences with the same pattern as the example.
1. Prompt: he / break / promise
   Example: He never broke a promise.
    a. the young man / break / promise / so
    b. you / make / promise / and then break
    c. government / break / promise / provide / house
2. Prompt: he / not / be supposed to / pick up
   Example: He wasn't supposed to pick up people with me in the vehicle.
    a. people / not / be supposed to / drive / while
    b. we / not / be supposed to / cut / tree / otherwise

      c. you / be supposed to / report / accident

3. Prompt: I / barely / notice

    Example: But I was six or seven and was barely noticed.

    a. apartment / barely / furnish / so

    b. village / barely / affect / flood / because

    c. she / earn / barely / money to

4. Prompt: he / stay / on his own

    Example: he'd stay on his own, work even longer hours and live on sandwiches and tea.

    a. my son / on his own / never / ask / money

    b. old people / would rather / on their own / than

    c. my father / tell me / I / live / on my own

5. Prompt: man / say / little / stare at / baby / me

    Example: This extraordinary man said very little, just stared at the baby and then at me.

    a. my husband / stare at / me / as if

    b. impolite / stare at / stranger

    c. she / sit / motionless / stare at

PART 3   Extended Activities

1 ▷ Dictation

2 ▷ Read more

A Father, a Son and an Answer

    Passing through an airport one morning, I caught one of those trains that travels from the main terminal to their boarding gates. Free, sterile and impersonal, the trains run back and forth all day long. Not many people consider them fun, but on this Saturday I heard laughter.

At the front of the first car — looking out the window at the track that lay ahead — were a man and his son. We had just stopped to let off passengers, and the doors were closing again. "Here we go ! Hold on to me tight!" the father said. The boy, about five years old, made sounds of sheer delight.

"Look out there!" the father said to his son. "See that pilot? I bet he's walking to his plane." The son craned his neck to look.

As I got off, I remembered something I'd wanted to buy in the terminal. I was early for my flight, so I decided to go back.

Notes

1. one of those trains that take travellers from the main terminal to their boarding gates: These are shuttle trains that take passengers from the main terminal to where they board planes. In many Chinese airports, shuttle buses do the same job. The main terminal is the main building at an airport, where airport administration offices, ticket office, operation control, etc. are located.

2. mock-exasperated: pretending to be annoyed or impatient

3. shuttle: a vehicle travels back and forth over an established, often short route

4. soullessness: lack of sensitivity or the capacity for deep feeling

5. obscenities: expressions, dirty words or immoral action that are considered rude, offensive

6. civility: courteous behavior; politeness

I did — and just as I was about to reboard the train for my gate, I saw that the man and his son had returned too. I realized then that they hadn't been heading for a flight, but had just been riding the shuttle for fun.

"You want to go home now?" the father asked.

"I want to ride some more!"

"More?" the father said, mock-exasperated but clearly pleased, "You're not tired?"

"This is fun!" his son said.

"All right," the father replied, and when a door opened we all got on.

There are parents who can afford to send their children to Europe or Disneyland, and the children turn out rotten. There are parents who live in million-dollar houses and give their children cars and swimming pools, yet something goes wrong. Rich and poor, so much goes wrong so often.

"Where are all these people going, Daddy?" the son asked.

"All over the world," came the reply. The other people in the airport were leaving for distant destinations or arriving at the ends of their journeys. The father and son, though, were just riding this shuttle together, making it exciting, sharing each other's company.

There are so many troubles — crime, the murderous soullessness that seems to be taking over the lives of many young people, the lowering of educational standards, the increase in vile obscenities in public, the disappearance of simple civility. So many questions about what to do. Here was a father who cared about spending the day with his son and who had come up with this plan on a Saturday morning.

The answer is so simple: parents who care enough to spend time, pay attention to the needs of their children, and try their best. It costs nothing, yet it is the most valuable thing in the world.

The train picked up speed, and the father pointed something out, and the boy laughed again, and the answer is so simple.

A True / False / Not Mentioned (NM).

1. The train the narrator caught ran from downtown to the airport.
2. The father in the story took his son with him in the train because he was the engineer driver.
3. The author took the train twice because he thought that riding on a train is fun.
4. As the son kept asking questions, the father became a little annoyed.
5. The father and son didn't like to live in a million-dollar house or have expensive cars or swimming pools.
6. Both the father and son enjoyed their shuttle trip.
7. The father and son were going to board a plane.
8. In the narrator's opinion, many troubles of young people today are due to lack of care and love on the part of the parents.

B Topics for discussion.

An English proverb says: "Spare the rod and spoil the child." By contrast, the text tells us a story of a loving father. Which, do you think, is the better way in bringing up a child? Give your reasons.

3 ▶ Grammar work

Correct the mistakes in the following sentences.

1. I would live in Nanjing when I was at primary school.
2. The explorer discovered the ancient cave in accident.
3. This course requires that every student turn in a paper of two pages least and four pages most.
4. Debbie is not sometimes responsible for what she does.
5. Nobody knows the exact age of the earth by certain.
6. He raised his arm to protect his face to the blow.
7. The beggar accepted the food and money and gave a performance as return.
8. A stitch on time saves nine.
9. The postman dropped my letter into our neighbor's mail box through mistake.
10. He sent his parcel by the sea since airmail was too expensive.

4 ▶ Word formation

Fill in the following blanks with derivatives of the words in the brackets.

1. No one could account for the _____ (remove) of the desk from the room.
2. I know you don't like him, but at least have the _____ (decent) to be polite to him in public.
3. Of course it's _____ (moral) to cheat people.
4. What annoys me is her complete _____ (regard) for anyone else's opinion.
5. She'd be better at her job as a jailer if she could _____ (hard) her heart.
6. We are hoping to _____ (final) the arrangements with the members of the committee.
7. When I was at school, we were required to _____ (memory) a poem every week.
8. You must _____ (capital) the first letter of the first word of a sentence in writing.

> *-ise / -ize* is very often used to make new transitive verbs from nouns or adjectives with the meaning of *causing to be*, or *make*. For example, to modernize our country is to make her modern; to privatize the enterprise is to put it into private ownership; to finalize the agreement between the two parties means to cause it to be completed. The form *-ise* is more common in British English than in American English. However, the following words must be spelt with *-ise*: advertise, compromise, improvise, merchandise, since they are not formed in the *n / adj +-ise* formula.

5 ▶ Vocabulary work

Choose the correct phrase to explain the underlined part.

1. Joe and I <u>have a good relationship</u>.
   a. get on well with each other
   b. know each other fairly well
   c. are in love with each other

2. Adrian and Liz <u>don't see eye to eye</u>.
   a. don't see each other very often
   b. are different in height
   c. often disagree and argue

3. John <u>has fallen out</u> with his parents again.
   a. has had a fight
   b. has been beaten by
   c. has had arguments

4. Tony and Jane <u>have broken up</u>.
   a. have had an accident and are injured
   b. have ended their relationship
   c. have run away

5. Children should respect their <u>elders</u>.

    a. old people

    b. adults or parents

    c. young brothers and sisters

6. Let's try to <u>make up</u>.

    a. be friends again

    b. play a game

    c. make us prettier

7. She's my <u>junior</u>, so she does what she's told.

    a. younger sister

    b. lower in grade at school

    c. classmate

6 Translation

Put the following sentences into English.

1. 老师告诉我瓶里的液体可以去除金属和瓷器上的污渍。**remove**

2. 坐在我旁边的学生忐忑不安地看着考场的四周。**apprehension**

3. 他现在大学毕业了，自己养活自己。**on his own**

4. 他们轮流睡觉，以免出差错。**go wrong**

5. 大女儿也许会接父亲的班，等她长大后接管家业。**follow in one's footsteps**

6. 他不得不跳下自行车，推车上山。**get off**

7. 这副手套将保护你的手不受冻。**protect**

7 Writing

A Work on your own.

The narrator repeats "he was my father / dad" several times. Add one more sentence after that to explain what each sentence means:

1. He was my father. (2nd paragraph) _____

2. ... he was my dad. (5th paragraph) _____

3. He was my father. (6th paragraph) _____

4. He was my father. (8th paragraph) _____

5. ... he was my father. (last paragraph) _____

B An extraordinary ordinary man.

The narrator calls his father an extraordinary ordinary man, which means his father is both extraordinary and ordinary. Find out from the story the points that show these

two features and fill them into the following grid.

Facts to show that the father was an extraordinary man. (You may start like this):	Facts to show that the father was an ordinary man. (You may start like this):
• a caring father, paying attention to his children's moral education	• a taxi driver, working 12 hours a day, six days a week in order to earn a decent wage

C ultural Information

 Read the passage below, and then complete the task of cultural study.

Family Structure in UK and US

The British and the Americans live longer, marry later, have fewer children, and are more likely to get divorced than ever before. Young people leave home earlier, though not necessarily to get married. More women now go out to work, and more people, especially the old, live alone. The nuclear family (parents and perhaps two children) has largely replaced the extended family where several generations live together.

Although patterns are changing, most people in Britain and the United States still get married and have children and stay together until the end of their lives. People are marrying later: the average woman in Britain gets married at twenty-four to a man who is just over two years older. In US, the average age at first marriage in 1994 was 24.5 years for women and 26.7 years for men. Nine out of ten married women in Britain will have children at some point in their lives. And despite the changes in working habits, it is usually the woman who has overall responsibility for domestic life: the traditional division of family responsibilities still persists.

Britain has one of the highest divorce rates in Western Europe: approximately one in three marriages breaks up in divorce, half of them in the first ten years of marriage. As a result, more people are getting remarried and there are now over a million single parents looking after 1.6 million children. In the United States, the divorce rate is also high. For the year 1995, for example, the number of marriages was about 2.3 million and that of divorce cases was over 1.1 million. Many households are single-parent families, mostly maintained by women. In 1994, there were 11.4 million single parents, among whom 9.9 million were single mothers. Children from single-parent families have less access to adult attention, less help with homework and less time with both parents than those with two-parent families. They were likely to drop out of school and fail in their future career.

 Cultural Study Task

Plan a study to find out the general situation about the marriage age in your local town or city. You may design a questionnaire and get information from about 10 respondents.

Understanding Your Owner

Introduction

In this unit, you will learn to use English for

▶ Expressing disapproval and dissatisfaction
▶ Discussing pet-keeping, and the issues of mutual understanding
▶ Fairy tales in English speaking cultures

PART 1 Communicative Activities

1 ▶ Interactive listening and speaking

A Listening

In this conversation you will hear two senior people, Peter and Nelson, talking about

pet-keeping. Listen, and answer the following questions.

1. What is the difference between Peter and Nelson in their attitudes to pet-keeping?
   a. Peter disapproves of treating animals like human beings, but Nelson doesn't think so.
   b. Nelson believes that pet-keeping is a natural need of human beings, but Peter doesn't think so.
   c. Nelson makes a distinction between human friends and animals, but Peter doesn't.
2. What's Peter's reason for keeping pets?
   a. He believes that animals like to make friends with human beings.
   b. He would not feel lonely if he keeps pets.
   c. Life is short, so he should love animals, too.
3. Which of the following animals does Peter now keep?
   a. A dog, a cat, goldfish.
   b. Goldfish, birds, a dog.
   c. Birds, a dog, a cat.
4. The conversation touches upon a big issue: mutual understanding. On this point, how are Peter and Nelson different from each other?
   a. Peter believes that it can only be found among human beings.
   b. Nelson believes that it can only be found between human beings and animals.
   c. It is not achievable.

B Communication

Communication is one of the important keys to achieve mutual understanding. But communication doesn't mean people always have to convey meaningful content in conversation. Study the following short drama in groups and then answer these questions:

1. What is the most striking characteristic of the conversation?
2. There is very little action, nor much thought in the conversation. But there is communication between the two men. What do they communicate actually?
3. Would they be happy with "more content"?
4. If so, what are they likely to talk about?
5. What motivates the two men to continue their fragmented conversation?

Last to Go
by Harold Pinter

A coffee stall. A BARMAN and an old NEWSPAPER SELLER. The BARMAN leans on his counter, the OLD MAN stands with tea.
Silence.

MAN:	You was a bit busier earlier.
BARMAN:	Ah.
MAN:	Round about ten.

BARMAN: Ten, was it?

MAN: About then.

Pause.

I passed by here about then.

BARMAN: Oh yes?

MAN: I noticed you were doing a bit of trade.

Pause.

BARMAN: Yes, trade was very brisk here about ten.

MAN: Yes, I noticed.

Pause.

I sold my last one about then. Yes. About nine forty-five.

BARMAN: Sold your last then, did you?

MAN: Yes, my last "Evening News" it was. Went about twenty to ten.

Pause.

BARMAN: "Evening News", was it?

MAN: Yes.

Pause.

Sometimes it's the "Star" is the last to go.

BARMAN: Ah.

MAN: Or the ... whatsisname.

BARMAN: "Standard".

MAN: Yes.

Pause.

All I had left tonight was the "Evening News".

Pause.

BARMAN: Then that went, did it?

MAN: Yes.

Pause.

Like a shot.

Pause.

BARMAN: You didn't have any left, eh?

MAN: No. Not after I sold that one.

Pause.

BARMAN: It was after that you must have come by here then, was it ?

MAN: Yes, I come by here after that, see, after I packed up.

BARMAN: You didn't stop here though, did you?

MAN: When?

BARMAN: I mean, you didn't stop here and have a cup of tea then, did you?

MAN: What, about ten?

BARMAN: Yes.

MAN: No, I went up to Victoria.

BARMAN: No, I thought I didn't see you.

MAN: I had to go up to Victoria.

A London Coffee Stall

Pause.

BARMAN: Yes, trade was very brisk here about then.

Pause.

MAN: I went to see if I could get hold of George.

BARMAN: Who?

MAN: George.

Pause.

BARMAN: George who?

MAN: George ... whatsisname.

BARMAN: Oh.

Pause.

Did you get hold of him?

MAN: No. No, I couldn't get hold of him. I couldn't locate him.

BARMAN: He's not about much now, is he?

Pause.

MAN: When did you last see him then?

BARMAN: Oh, I haven't seen him for years.

MAN: No, nor me.

Pause.

BARMAN: Used to suffer very bad from arthritis.

MAN: Arthritis?

BARMAN: Yes.

MAN: He never suffered from arthritis.

BARMAN: Suffered very bad.

Pause.

MAN: Not when I knew him.

Pause.

BARMAN: I think he must have left the area.

Pause.

MAN: Yes, it was the "Evening News" was the last to go tonight.

BARMAN: Not always the last though, is it, though?

MAN: No. Oh no. I mean sometimes it's the "News". Other times it's one of the others. No way of telling beforehand. Until you've got your last one left, of course. Then you can tell which one it's going to be.

BARMAN: Yes.

Pause.

MAN: Oh yes.

Pause.

I think he must have left the area.

Notes

1. Pinter, H. (1930–2008), modern British playwright, 2005 Nobel prize laureate in literature.
2. The play *Last to Go* is one of Pinter's most famous short plays, in which a barman and a newspaper seller chat idly about a variety of pointless topics which probably mean nothing to either of them.
3. You was a bit busier earlier: non-standard English dialect
4. Evening News, Star and The Standard: three of London evening newspapers (at the time when the play was written)
5. Whatsisname: (dialect) What is its / his name?
6. Like a shot: (The last copy) was sold quickly.
7. Packed up: pack up his bags or luggage (to finish his business)
8. Victoria: a district, and an important railway station in London
9. He's not about much now: He isn't around here for a long time.

C Activities

Study the following episodes taken from the play, and modify them into a meaningful talk. You may also modify the language into Standard English. The first one has been done as an example.

Old conversation	Your new conversation
Example: **Episode 1** MAN: You was a bit busier earlier. BARMAN: Ah. MAN: Round about ten. BARMAN: Ten, was it? MAN: About then. *Pause.* I passed by here about then. BARMAN: Oh yes? MAN: I noticed you were doing a bit of trade. *Pause.* BARMAN: Yes, trade was very brisk here about ten. MAN: Yes, I noticed. *Pause.* I sold my last one about then. Yes. About nine forty-five.	MAN: Hey, man. Good business, isn't it? BARMAN: Hi, yes. It's good. How are you doing? MAN: Not bad. I was passing by just now, and noticed you had good business. BARMAN: Oh, man. I didn't see you. When did you pass by? MAN: It's about ten. BARMAN: Yes. Trade was very brisk here about ten. How is your newspaper business today? MAN: My business is OK. I sold my last one about ten ... (The two men sound in high spirits.)
Episode 2 BARMAN: Yes, trade was very brisk here about ten. MAN: Yes, I noticed. *Pause.* I sold my last one about then. Yes. About nine forty-five. BARMAN: Sold your last then, did you? MAN: Yes, my last "Evening News" it was. Went about twenty to ten. *Pause.* BARMAN: "Evening News", was it? MAN: Yes. *Pause.* Sometimes it's the "Star" is the last to go. BARMAN: Ah. MAN: Or the ... whatsisname. BARMAN: "Standard". MAN: Yes. *Pause.* All I had left tonight was the "Evening News". *Pause.* BARMAN: Then that went, did it? MAN: Yes. *Pause.* Like a shot. *Pause.* BARMAN: You didn't have any left, eh? MAN: No. Not after I sold that one.	

Episode 3

BARMAN: It was after that you must have come by here then, was it?

MAN: Yes, I come by here after that, see, after I packed up.

BARMAN: You didn't stop here though, did you?

MAN: When?

BARMAN: I mean, you didn't stop here and have a cup of tea then, did you?

MAN: What, about ten?

BARMAN: Yes.

MAN: No, I went up to Victoria.

BARMAN: No, I thought I didn't see you.

MAN: I had to go up to Victoria.

Pause.

BARMAN: Yes, trade was very brisk here about then.

Pause.

Episode 4

MAN: I went to see if I could get hold of George.

BARMAN: Who?

MAN: George.

Pause.

BARMAN: George who?

MAN: George ... whatsisname.

BARMAN: Oh.

Pause.

Did you get hold of him?

MAN: No. No, I couldn't get hold of him. I couldn't locate him.

BARMAN: He's not about much now, is he?

Pause.

MAN: When did you last see him then?

BARMAN: Oh, I haven't seen him for years.

MAN: No, nor me.

Pause.

BARMAN: Used to suffer very bad from arthritis.

MAN: Arthritis?

BARMAN: Yes.

MAN: He never suffered from arthritis.

BARMAN: Suffered very bad.

Pause.

MAN: Not when I knew him.

Pause.

BARMAN: I think he must have left the area.

Pause.

Episode 5

    MAN: Yes, it was the "Evening News" was the last to go tonight.

BARMAN: Not always the last though, is it, though?

    MAN: No. Oh no. I mean sometimes it's the "News". Other times it's one of the others. No way of telling beforehand. Until you've got your last one left, of course. Then you can tell which one it's going to be.

BARMAN: Yes.

    Pause.

    MAN: Oh yes.

    Pause.

    I think he must have left the area.

Proverb

It takes two to make a quarrel.

PART 2 Reading and Language Activities

Text Understanding Your Owner

▶ Pre-reading tasks **Discuss the following question.**

Study the following cartoon. What comment do you want to make?

➤ Do you believe that dogs can understand human beings? Read the following article.

Although I know that many of you think the opposite, most human beings have a high level of intelligence, a good memory and can solve problems easily. They live longer and therefore tend to be much more aware of past and future than we are. They communicate by a set of sounds which carry meaning from the order in which they are placed. And these sounds vary from territory to territory, so that some humans have difficulty in communicating with others — if they have been raised in a different country and have not had special training. Humans have also invented a set of marks on paper which they use to represent these sounds and which you may often see them concentrating on. In these two ways they have developed their eyes and ears to a higher level of interpretation than we dogs. But in doing so they have lost the ability to get much of the information which we continually do both from these and our other senses.

Most dogs are able to interpret at least part of the vocabulary (voice meanings) of humans, and some of us have learnt to recognize some of the pattern of marks which they use to record them on paper so that humans at a different time and in a different place can understand their messages. But it would put our other abilities in danger if we ourselves developed these skills very far. Fortunately, most humans are able to understand a similar amount of our communicatory sounds and behavior.

Try going up to a human, sitting down in front of him and raising a front paw in a gesture. He will almost certainly take it and give it a shake, because it is a greeting gesture for humans, too. He will think you are behaving like a human — and nothing seems to please humans more.

Careful, there is a danger here! You are not a human. You are a dog — and if you are going to be happy you should never forget it. You need to live as a dog. It is all very well changing yourself slightly to fit in with a human pack, but if you deny your true nature, you are going to end up a mad dog and, humans will think, a bad dog. There is always a reason for any animal choosing to live with an animal of a different sort, but all too often we have no choice. We have to live with humans and we have to join a pack that is forced on us , so there is not much you can do about it. But humans have consciously decided that they want us with them although not necessarily for the reasons that they believe. They may need a dog to help with some specific task like hunting or guiding. They may want you as a watchdog to keep burglars away. They may have some idea that looking after you will teach their pups a sense of responsibility. They may just want you to make other humans look at them because your breed is expensive and fashionable. Or they may simply be in desperate need of companionship, of something to love.

1 Comprehension work

A Questions for discussion.

1. Who is the "owner" in the title?

2. What does the phrase "a set of sounds" mean? Why do some humans have difficulty communicating with others by using a set of sounds?

3. What does the phrase "a set of marks on paper" mean? What is the use of the marks for human beings?

4. Why shouldn't a dog develop the same communicating means / skills as human beings?

5. According to the passage, what is the best policy for a dog to live peacefully with human beings?

6. What are the reasons that human beings keep a dog as a pet?

B Activity

The article Understanding Your Owner is written from a dog's perspective. Read it again to find out the places where the author is trying to create a humorous effect, and comment on its effectiveness of the humorous style.

Places where the humor is created	Your comments on effectiveness
For example Although I know that many of you think the opposite, most human beings have a high level of intelligence, a good memory and can solve problems easily.	The writer did not speak highly of human beings at the beginning, even from a dog's point of view. By saying "think the opposite", the author wants to express a humorous evaluation of human intelligence, memory, and problem solving ability. They are only high from this particular dog's perspective.

2 Language work

A Fill in the following blanks with the words from the text.

1. Human beings have _____ a great fondness for dogs. This fondness has its historical and religious reasons. Since early times, dogs have become the most faithful friends

to _____. They can help with different _____, and even save people from _____ dangers.

2. In contact with human beings, most dogs have understood a large _____ of messages from human behavior: nodding, waving, facial expression and some greeting _____. In addition, they have learnt to _____ the meanings of human language. From the voice of their _____, dogs can tell whether the human is pleased, annoyed or angry. Besides, some dogs can _____ the written marks after some _____. They may know what meanings these marks and symbols _____.

3. Police dogs are normally of an expensive _____. They can demonstrate a high level of _____, which can help the police solve some difficult problems in _____ situations. They can _____ information or clues not available to human beings with their extraordinary _____ of smelling and hearing.

4. It has been suggested that the people who feel lonely and need some sort of _____ had better keep some small domestic animals as pets. But some people go so far as to _____ themselves all other pleasures and interests. Pets have turned out to be the only beloved ones of those people.

B Find these phrases in the text and make sure you know their meanings.

fit in with	a high level (of)	vary from … to …	all too
much more	in need of	at least part of	very far
keep away	end up	a sense of responsibility	a similar amount

Work with your partners. Take turns to choose a sentence from column A and respond with an appropriate sentence from column B.

A	B
1. The boy has soon made a lot of friends in the new school.	a. Yes, "One apple a day keeps the doctor away."
2. Bio-technology has developed to a very high level.	b. Yes, at least a person with a sense of responsibility.
3. Fresh fruits are good for people's health.	c. Yes. They're always over all too soon.
4. People feel very uncomfortable with the temperature here.	d. Yes, at least part of it isn't affected at all.
5. The boxer did not practice a lot.	e. Yes. But it would be dangerous if it goes very far.
6. The building was only slightly damaged in the fire.	f. Yes. He ended up a loser.
7. The project is in need of an earnest assistant.	g. Yes. He can quickly fit in with the new environment.
8. The holidays went much more quickly than I had expected.	h. Yes. It varies from 40°C at noon to 0°C at night.

C Word study.

a. **Give the meanings of the following words or expressions used in the text. You may use an English-English Dictionary. Then give a sentence to illustrate their meanings and usage.**

1. be aware of

    _____

2. vary from ... to

    _____

3. end up

    _____

4. force on

    _____

5. desperate

    _____

6. companionship

    _____

b. **Each of the following clues has an example sentence. Use the prompts to produce other sentences with the same pattern as the example.**

1. Prompt: they / be aware of / past and future

    Example: They tend to be much more aware of past and future than we are.

    a. be aware of / risk / we / give up / project

    b. be aware of / mistake / he / apologize / and / ask for / forgiveness

    c. teachers / be aware of / difficulties of students

2. Prompt: they / communicate / sound / vary from ... to

    Example: They communicate by a set of sounds which vary from territory to territory.

    a. message / convey / gesture / vary from ... to

    b. income / vary from ... to / in the company / depend on / one's performance / rather than / age

    c. meaning of smiles / vary from ... to / culture

3. Prompt: deny / true nature / you / end up

    Example: If you deny your true nature, you are going to end up a mad dog.

    a. I / be told / if / not work hard / end up

    b. we / not / surprise / he / end up / burglar

    c. because of / poor management / project / end up a wreck

4. Prompt: we / join / pack / force on

    Example: We have to join a pack that is forced on us.

    a. women / put up with / inequality / force on

    b. China / not accept / treaties / force on

    c. students / complain about / excessive work / force on

5. Prompt: they / be / desperate / companionship

Example: They may simply be in desperate need of companionship.

a. old people / lonely / desperate / companionship

b. young woman / have another baby / only son / desperate / companionship

c. psychiatrist / say / nothing wrong with the patient / just in desperate need of / companionship

PART 3 Extended Activities

1 ▶ Dictation

2 ▶ Read more

A Tracker Dog

"Track!" said my master.

Like any obedient tracker-dog who had received the command he most loves, I gave a bark of excitement, put my nose down to the pavement and sniffed.

A small group of people gathered behind us. Among these onlookers was the old caretaker of the building next door to ours. He spoke in a scornful voice: "You actually think your dog might catch a thief three days after the event?"

My master said nothing, but I'm sure he must have smiled. I did not turn to look. I knew he would not speak unless it was to give me a new command.

I needed to concentrate. My task was difficult. I had to pick out one scent among the many that lay about and then track it to its source.

"I've seen many tracker-dogs in my time," said the caretaker to the onlookers. "I served with the police years ago. We would never have thought of using a tracker-dog to find a car thief. Impossible. Everyone knows that dogs are useless in such matters. He's got his car back, so what's the use of parking it again in the same place and trying to pick up one scent among the hundreds on this pavement? It's like asking the dog to do a crossword puzzle!"

In a sense he was right. I'm sure there's no need to tell you that, just as a dog's hearing is much better than a human being's, so his sense of smell distinguishes one thing from another far better than the most powerful magnifying glass in the world. If Sherlock Holmes could work out that a man had had an egg for breakfast by seeing the yellow stain on his mouth, a trained dog could tell you whether the hen that laid the egg was healthy or not.

I know it sounds funny and I mean it to be. But I'm not exaggerating. A dog can tell you — provided you understand a dog's way of communicating — all this and more without even setting eyes on the man he is investigating. But here the ground was criss-crossed in a complex knot of different smells and scents and tracks. To untie it and follow one of them, seemed like asking for a miracle.

Notes

1. tracker dog: a tracker dog is a kind of dog which can help people by following footprints or other signs that show where they have been
2. criss-crossed: marked with lines crossing each other
3. Sherlock Holmes: A detective in stories by English writer Sir Arthur Conan Doyle (1859–1930). He is well-known for his extraordinary ability to solve mysteries.
4. in a sense: to some extent

A Choose the best answer to each of the following questions.

1. What did the dog-narrator feel about tracking?
   A. It did what was asked because it was obedient.
   B. It was excited, even though it wasn't a special tracker-dog.
   C. It was frustrated because it shouldn't concentrate properly.
   D. It found tracking difficult, but enjoyed it.

2. What did the caretaker think about using a dog to catch a thief?
   A. He was hopeful and encouraging towards the dog's owner.
   B. He was doubtful because of his previous experience with tracker-dogs.
   C. He was envious because in the police they had never come up with the idea.
   D. He thought that what most people say isn't necessarily right.

3. What do we learn about the dog-owner and his car?
   A. He was trying to find his car, which had been stolen three days before.
   B. His car had not been stolen but he was using it to catch a car thief.
   C. His car had been stolen three days before but now it had been found.
   D. He had found part of his car and was using the dog to try to find the rest.

4. What does the dog-narrator tell us about its sense of smell?
   A. It is not so good as its sense of hearing.

B. It can achieve what a human's sight can and much more.

C. It can only give us more details about what a human has already discovered.

D. When there are many scents together, it cannot distinguish one from another.

5. According to the passage, a dog can _____.

   A. give you a lot of information if you can communicate with it

   B. tell you many things without seeing you

   C. provide you with a way of communicating with it

   D. do more than just investigate what people can't see

B Topics for discussion.

1. Did the dog-narrator in the text fulfil its task?

2. Why do people use tracker-dogs to search for a thief?

3. What can a tracker-dog do and not do?

3 Grammar work

Correct the mistakes in the following sentences.

1. Bob denied to break the window, but I'm sure he did.

2. I remember to have closed the door. But I'm not sure if I locked it or not.

3. Let's face it. It's no good to worry any more tonight.

4. Judy was finally tired of having quarrelled with her husband.

5. I'm sorry to keep on cough all the time.

6. Though the job was not easy, she did not regret to accept the offer.

7. We have been in the same department for quite a few years. Now we are used to work together.

8. I can't help to feel that it was a mistake to let her go.

9. I'm looking forward to see you again in Beijing.

10. Excuse me to interrupt. Have you mentioned a Jones, Jones what?

4 Word formation

Fill in the following blanks with derivatives of the words in the box.

apprehension	heaven	collect	act	cost
true	home	scholar	support	co-operate

1. We have to take _____ action if we want to prevent more serious mistakes from happening.

2. From the very start, Benjamin was an _____ member in the club.

3. It would be too _____ to repair that old car.

4. We spent a _____ day on the beach.

5. I felt a bit _____ about the operation.

6. The teachers tried to train the students to be _____ in class activities.

7. She was helping them in a strongly _____ way.

8. A lot of people end their letter with "_____" instead of "sincerely."

9. We stayed in *Hotel of Golden Sand*, a _____ and comfortable place.

10. Do you know that _____ young man? He actually is a professor in our university.

Suffix *-ive* can form adjectives from verbs, giving a meaning of "*having a tendency*" or "*the quality of*," e.g. *explosive*.

-ly is a suffix for forming adverbs from adjectives: e.g. *gladly*. In addition, it can be used to form adjectives from nouns, meaning "every", e.g. *hourly*. Sometimes, it is used as an adjectival suffix meaning "like", e.g. *manly*.

---

5 ▷ Vocabulary work

Combine the sentence in column A with the phrase in column B with a suitable preposition so that they make sense. The first one has been done for you.

1. Everyone praised him for → c.	a. clients' credibility.
2. Many children have trouble concentrating	b. making a new machine.
3. I have to stay at home and prepare	c. playing so well in the game.
4. She has made a tremendous effort and succeeded	d. the math test tomorrow.
5. Whether or not a bank will grant a loan depends	e. doing their school work.
	f. Winston Churchill.
6. It was an awful hotel and we complained	g. his performance in the concert.
7. This house reminded me	h. its poor service.
8. We congratulated him	i. a place I used to know.
9. I can't forgive him	j. telling lies and cheating in the exam.
10. They named their son	

---

6 ▷ Translation

Put the following sentences into English.

1. 起初他拒绝承担任何责任，但最后他终于道歉了。**end up**

2. 有时要从人群中认出一个熟人是不容易的。**pick out**

3. 有些方便食品符合当今健康饮食的观点。**fit in with**

4. 你的轻率行事，可能会使我们遇到危险。**put ... into danger**

5. 他想将他的主张强加于我们，但我们没有接受。**force on**

47

6. 他们花了好几个小时才得出调查的结果。**work out**

7. 如果你这样做不行，可以试一试其他方法。**try+v-ing**

8. 她病了，几个星期都不能工作。**keep off**

 7 ▶ **Writing**

A Working from a dog's point of view.

Explain the following words or expressions from a dog's point of view. Pay attention to the tone of phrases so that they sound like a dog's opinion.

1. spoken language

_____

2. written language

_____

3. greeting such as saying "hello"

_____

4. studying a course like what people do at school

_____

5. a good dog

_____

6. educating children

_____

7. social vanity

_____

8. reading

_____

B Write a short paragraph on the following topic.

What can a pet owner learn from the story "Understanding Your Owner"?

C ultural Information

Read the passage below, and then complete the task of cultural study.

Fairy Tales

A fairy tale is a traditional story whose events are magically caused. The best known fairy tales in the West are the works of the brothers Grimm (Grimm's fairy tales) and Anderson. The most modern fairy tales are Walt Disney's animated stories. The following is a brief list of fairy tales known to almost all the children in the English speaking countries, or even world-wide.

- *Alice in Wonderland* — a story by Lewis Carroll, in which a little girl called Alice falls down a rabbit hole and comes to a magic land where many strange animals and people appear and funny things happen.
- *Peter Pan* — a story by J. M. Barrie, in which a young boy, Peter Pan, who never grows up, lives in a magic land called Never-Never Land where he and his friends Michael, John and Wendy and the fairy, Tinkerbell have many adventures.
- *Robin Hood* — a hero in many old stories, who lived as an outlaw in Sherwood Forest, near Nottingham, with a group of companions (the Merry Men). He is remembered especially for stealing money from rich people and giving it to poor people.
- *The Legend of Sleepy Hollow* — a story by American writer Washington Irving in which the main character, Ichabod Crane, is frightened by what he thinks is a headless man riding a horse.
- *Harry Potter* — a series of seven fantasy novels written by British author J. K. Rowling. The series chronicles the adventure of a young wizard named Harry Potter, his best friends Ron Weasley, and Hermione Granger, all of whom are Harry's classmates at Hogwarts School of Witchcraft and Wizardry. The central story line is about Harry's struggle against the evil wizard Voldemort who murdered Harry's parents in his quest to conquer the wizarding world and subjugate the non-magical population.

Cultural Study Task

What are the well-known Chinese fairy tales? Ask 10 classmates to vote for a list. And write a short essay in about 200 words about the title, the author, and the synopsis of the story based on the survey.

Water Cycle

Introduction

In this unit, you will learn to use English for

▶ Expressing different degrees of certainties
▶ Talking about wastewater treatment and environmental protection
▶ Science / technology / resources' impact on environment

PART 1 Communicative Activities

1 ▶ Interactive listening and speaking

In this recording, you will hear an expert giving a lecture to a group of high school students about wastewater treatment technologies. Listen, take notes, and complete the following tasks.

1. Describe the process of water cycle according to the expert. Use the following clues for your description.
   a. Water in molecules
   b. Water in a stream
   c. Water in a reservoir
   d. Water in our bathtub sink or flush toilet
   e. Water in the wastewater treatment plant

2. Use your note to describe a sewer system which is called engineering marvel by the expert. Use the following clues for your description.
   a. Wastewater from millions of homes, business, industries and institutions
   b. Wastewater in transport
   c. Wastewater in destination

3. What is the closest estimate below for the water and waste material ratio in our used water from home?
   a. Half and half
   b. Majority of water, and the rest is the waste material
   c. Majority of waste material, and the rest is water

4. Describe how the three major steps work in treating wastewater based on what you have heard. Use the following clues for your description.
   a. Preliminary Step
   b. Primary Step
   c. Secondary Step
   d. Mechanical Processes
   e. Biological Processes
   f. Chemical Processes

5. Based on what you have heard from the expert, explain the nature's processes of wastewater treatment. How does it seem to be different from the engineering processes in the wastewater treatment plant?

6. What is the byproduct of wastewater treatment? Describe one of the uses that the expert has mentioned in his lecture.

7. What feature have you noticed in the use of language for describing scientific and technological knowledge?

2 ▷ Expressing different degrees of certainties

Unlike talking about established scientific knowledge such as wastewater treatment, speaking about a topic in everyday life would require us to use a variety of means to show different degrees of certainties. Read the following sentences, and match them with the actual words spoken.

Actual words spoken	Functions
a. Are you quite sure you will have done your homework by tomorrow afternoon?	1. Say you are almost sure that he has missed the train.
b. He must've missed the 6:30 train.	2. Say you are not sure about which clothes to wear.
c. I'll finish my work on time. I give you my word for it.	3. Say you are sure you can finish your work on time.
d. I'll bet he's back home.	4. Say you are not sure if you will go or not.
e. I can't make up my mind whether to go or to stay.	5. Say you are sure he has come back.
f. I haven't a clue about what we should wear for the party.	6. Ask your friend if he is certain that he can finish his homework in time.

3   More sentences

Read the following sentences that are frequently used and complete the matching exercise.

1. I'm quite positive that our team will win the match this time.

2. I'm a hundred per cent certain Jane has flown to South Africa.

3. I have a feeling we've taken a wrong road, but I may not be correct.

4. I'm in two minds where to put my new TV.

5. You can be sure about their interest in this plan.

6. I've no doubt that you'll come out first in the contest.

7. I'm quite convinced of her experience in such a task.

8. I can't say for certain what to do next.

Matching Exercise

Divide the above sentences into the following two categories:

Sentences of Certainty: _____

Sentences of Uncertainty: _____

Proverb

The unexpected always happens.

PART 2 Reading and Language Activities

Text   Wizards of the Water Cycle

▶ Pre-reading tasks **Discuss the following questions.**

1. How much do you know about Singapore?
2. What else are you interested to know about this little city-state?

▶ Read the text

**Singapore's toilet-to-tap technology has saved the country
from shortages — and a large electricity Bill**

By Sandra Upson

When Singapore became independent in 1965 it faced an immediate challenge of water resources because the city-state has no groundwater. To address the problem, the government negotiated treaties with its neighbor country Malaysia to build a supply pipe at a cost to provide fresh water to this port city.

Sixty years later, the city-state has both gained territorial independence, and managed to bootstrap its way to wealth in spite of a lack of water and energy. (1)_____.

Rather than flushing waste into the sea, the water utility collects the country's wastewater, cleans it to pristine levels, and returns it to the public supply. (2)_____. Singapore has thus short-circuited the water cycle by reducing it to an island-ringing loop.

At first no one relished the idea of drinking wastewater. Rejuvenating the waste stream requires electricity to power an intensive cleaning process, and that investment makes the recycled water more expensive than what's used by cities blessed with nearby freshwater lakes, rivers, and aquifers. (3)_____.

What the utility did was a radical thing. After half a decade of research and tests at a pilot recycling plant, Singapore's planners unveiled their ultimate strategy for water security. (4)_____. They would force wastewater through filters under high pressure to remove all microbes, viruses, and larger impurities. With great emphasis on its sparkling purity, treated wastewater made its public debut in 2003.

The real work was about to start. One by one, the utility cajoled its customers into accepting the water. Manufacturers wondered what residues the water might have left on their wafers in their factories, but the utility pointed out that the ultrapure water was cleaner than most drinking water. Finally the island's 12 wafer-fabrication plants and other electronics manufacturers championed the ultrapure water, using it to wash their silicon wafers. (5)_____.

Singapore also started priming the public. The prime minister drank a bottle of the treated water at a national festival, and the crowd cheered. The message was clear — patriotic Singaporeans drink wastewater. (6)_____. A parody of a popular nationalist song, "Count on Me, Singapore," cheerily urged residents to "Drink Our Pee, Singapore."

The queasy reactions of some Singaporeans didn't deter the water utility. More water treatment plants are being built now, and by the end of this year, they will treat enough sewage to cover nearly a third of Singapore's water needs.

However, purifying water by this ultrapure technology means using a considerable amount of energy to make it, clean it, and move it. (7)_____ Because Singapore must import some 290 billion cubic feet of natural gas to run its power plants, it can be said that the country has merely substituted one form of dependence for another.

The solution to making the trade-off work, according to experts, is purely economic: Singapore charges all its customers the additional cost for purifying extra water. (8)_____. Experts are optimistic about the future. "New technologies come from everywhere," as one expert pointed out, "but our value is how we can exploit them to our best interest."

Notes

1. Sandra Upson: a technological writer for a science journal
2. the water utility: the management department of public water, power or gas supplies
3. aquifers: reservoirs in the rock or sand to hold fresh water
4. to bootstrap its way to wealth: (metaphorically) become wealthy independently; Cf. the phrase by one's bootstraps, meaning one did something all by one's own efforts, or independently.
5. at a cost: suffering a loss (in order to have something). When people say that they pay some money for something, it means that they have it at cost (i.e. not free); when they say that they buy or sell something at cost, it means that they buy or sell it for the amount of the money they get it or need it. However, when they say that they have something at a cost, it means that it is not cheap for them to have it and it may have cost them some loss.
6. short-circuited: cut a route short
7. an island-ringing loop: the water cycle (the loop) that takes place only on the island (i.e. Singapore), which implies that Singapore has stopped the natural process of water cycle involves evaporation, condensation (in the clouds) and precipitation (of rain falling back to the ground)
8. wafers: small, round thin silicon chips on which integrated circuits are made
9. optimize the juggle of resources: make best use of different kinds of resources (juggle: dealing with several alternatives at the same time)

Comprehension work

A Reading for coherence.

Insert the following sentences into appropriate blanks (There are more sentences than blanks.)

No.	Sentences	Locations
a	The question is how to optimize the juggle of resources.	
b	The companies calculated that the recycled water's exceeding purity saves them several billion a year, in part by cutting out steps in their internal water-purification process.	
c	And now, against all odds complete water independence — from both Malaysia and even the weather — is within easy reach.	
d	As a result, the water utility has enough cash to investigate new technologies.	
e	But presented with a set of tough choices, Singapore chose water recycling — and so far it has worked admirably.	
f	But the rest of Singapore was slower to follow.	

B Questions for discussion.

1. When Singapore became independent, what problems did it face in terms of resources, and how did it address these problems?

2. What is the trade-off of the wastewater treatment project? How did Singapore solve this problem? Do you think it is successful?

3. Read the following scientific report (**Task C Cloze**) on the situation of water supply in the world. What lessons can we draw from the Singaporean practice?

C Cloze

Fill in the blanks with suitable words.

> **Richest Water Countries**
>
> **World's Top Ten Nations for Freshwater Resources**
>
> Valued as much as US$700 billion per year, the global water market presents opportunities to countries with effective water infrastructures and supporting systems. The following list shows the estimated maximum amount of water (1) _____ to countries from both external and internal renewable sources.

The statistical summary gives a basic perspective on the ten (2) _____ countries in terms of the world's total freshwater resources, estimated at some 55,273 cubic kilometers per year (ckpy).

Ranks	Countries	Water amount available (ckpy)
1	Brazil	8,233 (14.9% of world total)
2	Russia	4,498 (8.1%)
3	Canada	3,300 (6%)
4	United States	3,069 (5.6%)
5	Indonesia	2,838 (5.1%)
6	China	2,830 (5.1%)
7	Columbia	2,132 (3.9%)
8	Peru	1,913 (3.5%)
9	India	1,908 (3.5%)
10	Democratic Republic of Congo	1,283 (2.3%)

The above 10 nations (3) _____ for about 60% of the world's total freshwater supply. But while these countries may be rich in water (4) _____, other studies rank a nation's water-richness by other factors.

Water Poverty Index

According to the World Water Forum, the international Water (5) _____ Index (WPI) scores the top 10 water-rich nations on 5 categories. The categories are: the size of a country's total water resources; how available those (6) _____ are to the population; how developed the country's water (7) _____ and delivery systems are; how efficiently or wastefully a country uses its water; and how well a country manages any environmental (8) _____ to its water.

Listed in ascending (9) _____ below are the countries scoring the highest marks on the WPI.

WPI ranks	Countries
1	Finland
2	Canada
3	Iceland
4	Norway
5	Guyana
6	Suriname
7	Austria
8	Ireland

9	Sweden
10	Switzerland

Many countries on the freshwater resources top 10 list are (10) _____ from the WPI top 10 list.

For example, America finished 32nd principally (11) _____ of inefficient or wasteful water use practices and because vast areas particularly in the American West are (12) _____ or semi-arid. The fact is that the US has the highest water consumption per capita in the world.

In (13) _____, smaller developing countries including Guyana and Suriname are much more effective in using their abundant water resources.

Global Water Supply

How important is it for countries including those with large freshwater supplies to improve their (14) _____ on the WPI?

According to some analysis, within 50 years, water shortages will (15) _____ half of the world's population living in 80 countries including America. Since water is costly to (16) _____ over long distances, countries are well-advised to manage their water resources and systems like Finland – and even Guyana and (17) _____.

(Based on Daniel Workman, http: / / www.suite101.com / content / richest-water-countries-a21701 (Jan 20, 2011))

2 ▶ Language work

Study the context in which these words are used, and then use them to write sentences with the given cues.

1) Address

To **address** the problem, the government negotiated treaties with its neighbor country Malaysia to build a supply pipe at a cost to provide fresh water to this port city.

(a) The problems of birds are so serious for the safety of the airport that scientists are determined to **address** them.

(b) Two writers **addressed** the issues of gay culture in the US army.

(c) Those problems are true, and you have to **address** them.

But **address** can be used in other ways. Read the usages below.

Usage 1

The teacher called for two volunteer students to help him **address** the envelopes at the preparation stage of the conference.

Usage 2

She ignored most of the people at the table, **addressing** only the man sitting next to her.

Usage 3

You should **address** the Queen as "Your Majesty".

> Now, write a meaningful sentence based on the given clues below.
> (a) address / professor / my buddy / surprise
> (b) address / audience / comedian / the meeting
> (c) official / failed to address / the needs / public transportation

2) **Cost**

Study the following examples:

(1) The original **cost** of the house was $200,000.

(2) By keeping the **costs** down, the company will make large profits this year.

(3) What are the **costs** and benefits of this new law?

(4) She was determined to win at all **costs**.

(5) They sold the books at **cost**.

(6) I found to my **cost** that he was a liar.

(7) She completed the project on time, but at the **cost** of her health.

> Now match the related interpretations of the meanings of cost in the above seven examples.
> a. disadvantage
> b. price for buying something
> c. expenses / money to run a business
> d. original amount for getting something
> e. damage / suffering
> f. bad experience
> g. anything — loss, damage or payment one has to bear
>
> Fill in the blanks with *cost*, *a cost*, *the cost*, *one's cost*, or *costs*.
> (a) Recovery has come at _____, however.
> (b) They developed a set of principles to assess the effectiveness, benefit, and _____ of new technologies.
> (c) The medicines listed on the categories will show _____, availability and complexity of use.
> (d) The renovation includes a brick house repair project at _____ of $700.
> (e) The project _____ was 500 Euros.
> (f) It's clear that the government did not understand the risks and _____ of the project they were taking on.
> (g) He found him, to _____, a dangerous political enemy.
> (h) The new management aims at increasing revenues and minimizing _____ of business operation.
> (i) Some people asked, "Should all patients be saved at any _____?" in the US national debate of medicare reform.

3) Champion

Study the examples in the left column with their definitions in the right one.

Sentences	Definitions
(1) People welcomed the Olympic **champions** at the airport. (2) He was a **champion** for working classes. (3) The political leader **championed** the idea to cut taxes.	(a) Someone has won a contest, especially in sports (b) Someone who speaks in public in support of certain ideas, rights, people (c) To speak publically in support of some ideas, rights, causes etc.

Write sentences based on the information on champion in the above table.
(a) Mr. Christie / positioned / champion / the middle class
(b) political leaders / champion / a more drastic social reform / small African country
(c) Mr. Blitz / lightweight boxing / champion / 1965's national boxing tournament

PART **3** Extended Activities

1 ▷ Dictation

2 ▷ Read more

Computers "Will Soon Jump to Our Every Word"

It's late evening in Munich station and you need a bed for the night. The tourist bureau is closed and there's no phone in sight. So what's new? Well, there's still the latest information system to try out.

Projected as an image on a wall in the station is a street map of the city and a set of icons. You point to the hotel icon and then circle with your finger the district you want. A more detailed street map, with flashing spots representing the hotels.

You point to one of the spots, and a list gives price and availability of rooms. You book by pointing to the telephone icon. A message on the wall tells you that a car is on its way to pick you up.

The fantasy could be a reality within a year or two, says Christopher Maggioni of a German electronics company. His research team at the company's laboratory in Munich has already built working prototypes. They remove the need to master tricky procedures on the keyboard, and leave little hardware on show for vandals to wreck. "These are the two great advantages," Mr. Maggioni says.

Notes

1. Munich: 慕尼黑 (德国城市)
2. tourist bureau: 旅游局
3. icons: 图标
4. on show: 展出
5. working prototype: 供试验用的样品
6. vandal: 破坏者
7. sterile environment: 无菌环境
8. desktop: 桌面
9. hospital operation theater: 医院
10. keypad: (电话) 号码键盘
11. furnishings: 装饰物
12. projector: 投影仪
13. 3D television: 立体影像电

"The systems are also fine for sterile environments and for clearing the office desktop." He sees doctors using gesture recognition systems in hospital operation theaters where unsterilized equipment is banned.

In the office, the clutter of telephones, diaries and address books on a desk could be a thing of the past. When you wanted to make a call, the image of a keypad could be projected on to the pile of papers beside you and you would move your fingers over the numbers as you do with a real telephone. Speakers and a microphone would be buried in the furnishings. For around $5 500 the system is also fairly cheap. It consists of a standard video camera and projector, and a computer.

For decades, researchers in US, Japan and Europe have been looking at ways of getting rid of the keyboard and of using gestures, voice and even eye movements to simplify the manner in which humans communicate with computers.

A number of companies claim to have built working prototypes of a computer system that recognizes head movements. This could be an important advance in the development of 3D television. Researchers now say that they can generate two images from a single screen and use a video camera to track the head to ensure that each image goes to the correct eye.

For Mr. Maggioni, the next big advance will be computers controlled by a combination of gestures and speech. Over the next few months, the company is due to launch a computer for the medical profession that will let doctors input data by talking to the machine, he says.

A True / False / Not Mentioned (NM).

1. Now the tourist bureau can provide accommodation information in late evening in Munich station.
2. In the new systems, a street map of the city is built on the wall.
3. To get information, you need to point to the hotel icon and then press a correct button.
4. The new systems are designed by a US electronics group.
5. One of the advantages of the systems is that surgeons can use them in an operation.
6. The new systems make the office look tidy and organized.
7. The new systems are more expensive than the old facilities.
8. A Japanese company has invented 3D television.

B Topics for discussion.

1. What is the difference between the new system in Munich station and the traditional one?
2. Why have researchers of computers been trying to get rid of the keyboard?
3. In what way have computers affected the lives of human beings?

  Grammar work

Correct the mistakes in the following sentences.

1. — What do you think will have happened by the end of the 21st century?
   — Scientists have discovered a cure for cancer. Or, oil and coal have been used up and new forms of energy have been discovered.
2. You may be in love with him now, but after a couple of weeks, he will have forgotten all about you.
3. By the time we get to New York we will drive over two hundred miles.
4. The seasons are predictable. For example, when spring is going to come, the weather gets warmer. This happens every year.
5. It has to rain because it's very dark outside now.
6. The museum will open at ten every morning.
7. According to the schedule, the mayor is going to deliver a speech on TV tomorrow evening.
8. He met her in the doorway just as she would go away.
9. If you swim this afternoon, you'd better get your swimming suit ready now.
10. Do you use the dictionary in the next lesson? I'd like to look up some words now.

4 Word formation

Fill in the following blanks with derivatives of the words in brackets.

1. The two colleges are _____ (operate) on the scientific research.
2. Since most of the schools in the district are going to participate in this _____ (school) competition, the organizing committee believe that the meeting will be a great success.

3. In the Film Festival, most foreign films are presented with Chinese _____ (titles).

4. She used to be very shy, but a year abroad has greatly _____ (form) her.

5. A _____ (marine) is a naval vessel that can operate underwater.

6. In US the underground is often called _____ (way), while in Britain people prefer to call it the tube.

7. The development of space technology makes it possible for people to have _____ (planetary) journeys from Earth to Mars.

8. His kidney can't work properly, so the doctor suggests _____ (plant) a new one in substitution.

9. John and I wrote the book jointly, so John is the _____ (author) of the book.

---

1. co- is a prefix added to adjectives, adverbs, nouns or verbs, meaning "together", "jointly", e.g. co-produced, co-driver , co-exist.

2. inter- is a prefix added to verbs, nouns or adjectives, meaning "between", "from one to another", e.g. international.

3. sub- is a prefix added to nouns or adjectives , meaning "under", "below", e.g. subsoil, submarine.

4. trans- is a prefix added to 1) adjectives, meaning "across" or "beyond", e.g. transatlantic, trans-Siberian; 2) verbs, meaning "into another place / state", e.g. transform.

---

5 ▷ Vocabulary work

Choose the suitable words of science and technology for the following blanks.

1. He _____ with a number of different materials before finding the right one.
   a. tested　　　　　　　b. experimented　　　　　c. examined

2. The technician pressed a button and lights started _____.
   a. bright　　　　　　　b. lightning　　　　　　　c. flashing

3. When she pulled a lever, the wheel began to _____.
   a. rotate　　　　　　　b. carry on　　　　　　　c. go on

4. The zoologist _____ the animal.
   a. opened　　　　　　　b. dissected　　　　　　　c. experimented

5. When they were mixed together, the two chemicals _____ violently with each other.
   a. worked　　　　　　　b. fought　　　　　　　　c. reacted

6. After analyzing the problem, the physicist concluded that there was a _____ in his initial hypothesis.
   a. hole　　　　　　　　b. wrong　　　　　　　　c. flaw

7. James Watt _____ the steam engine and Alexander Fleming, another Scot, discovered penicillin.
   a. invented　　　　　　b. discovered　　　　　　c. found

8. After switching on the computer, _____ a floppy disc into the disc drive.

   a. get into   b. invert   c. insert

9. You must _____ your invention as quickly as possible.

   a. copy   b. document   c. patent

6 Writing

The following diagram shows how wastewater is treated. Use what you have learned in this unit and elsewhere to write a passage describing a wastewater treatment process in about 200 words.

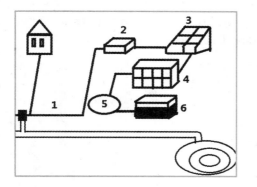

Cultural Information

Read the passage below, and then complete the task of cultural study.

Greenhouse Effects

The atmosphere is a blanket of gases around the earth. For thousands of years these gases have kept the planet's temperature at about 15°C. How? By trapping some of the sun's heat. But now, because of pollution, there are more and more hot gases released into the atmosphere. This means that Earth is getting hotter. A greenhouse becomes hot for the same reason. Its glass lets the sun's heat pass through, then stops some of it from leaving. That's why scientists call the problem of Earth's rising temperature "The Greenhouse Effect".

Most scientists agree that the Greenhouse Effect will add between 1.5 – 4°C to the Earth's temperature by 2030. This will change the weather everywhere. For example, the ice at the North and South Poles will start to melt. And when that happens the level of the sea will rise. If it rises one meter by 2030 there will be serious floods in many countries.

Then there is the problem of food. When the climate changes there will be less food in the world. At the moment, areas like the Midwest of America and central Russia grow a lot of wheat. In the future that may change when US and Russia become too dry for farming. Other countries (like Canada and Sweden) will become wetter, but that won't help. The soil there isn't rich. It won't be possible to grow the same amount of food as before.

We can't stop the Greenhouse Effect. However, we can slow it down if we use less fossil fuel, protect rain-forests, use more natural energy from the sun, sea and wind, and ban CFCs (chloro-fluoro-carbons = Freon 氟利昂) in our life.

 Cultural Study Task

Take a look at the surroundings where you are living and find out the places for environmental studies. Write your findings below to suggest at least three measures we can take to improve the efficiency of water and energy use in order to protect our environment.

(1) _____

(2) _____

(3) _____

Unit 5

Is My Team Ploughing

Introduction

In this unit, you will learn to use English for

- *Asking and answering questions*
- *Giving opinions and impressions*
- *Talking about issues of life such as work, play, friend and love*

PART 1 Communicative Activities

1 Interactive listening and speaking

A Read and speak.

In this section, you will read the poem *Is My Team Ploughing* written by the British poet A. E. Housman (1859 — 1936). Before you read, discuss the meanings of the words *team* and

ploughing **in the title. Which one of the following meanings might the poet use in the title?**

1) plough:

    a) The meaning in *The farmer ploughs the land.*

    b) The meaning in *The ship ploughs southward in the blue ocean.*

    c) The meaning in *The truck ploughs the road after the snow storm.*

2) team:

    a) a group of horses

    b) a person of extreme abilities

    c) a group of people

Pair work

The poem has eight stanzas in which two friends are asking and answering a series of questions. But the dialog is jumbled up in the picture below. Work with your partner to find out the correct sequence through speaking. You should take turns asking and answering the main idea in each stanza in your own words.

Is My Team Ploughing
By A.E. Housman

Ay, the horses trample,
    The harness jingles now;
No change though you lie under
    The land you used to plough.

"Is football playing
    Along the river shore,
With lads to chase the leather,
    Now I stand up no more?"

Ay, she lies down lightly,
    She lies not down to weep:
Your girl is well contented.
    Be still, my lad, and sleep.

"Is my friend hearty,
    Now I am thin and pine,
And has he found to sleep in
    A better bed than mine?"

Ay, the ball is flying,
    The lads play heart and soul,
The goal stands up, the keeper
    Stands up to keep the goal.

Yes, lad, I lie easy,
    I lie as lads would choose;
I cheer a dead man's sweetheart,
    Never ask me whose.

"Is my girl happy,
    That I thought hard to leave,
And has she tired of weeping
    As she lies down at eve?"

"Is my team ploughing,
    That I was used to drive
And hear the harness jingle
    When I was man alive?"

Write the poem here in its correct sequence.

_____
_____
_____
_____
_____
_____
_____
_____
_____
_____
_____
_____
_____
_____
_____
_____
_____
_____

Notes

1 Alfred Edward Housman (1859 — 1936), usually known as A. E. Housman, is an English classical scholar and poet, best known to the general public for his cycle of poems *A Shropshire Lad*.

2 chase the leather: chase the football

3 eve: (literary) evening

B Listening

Two students played a song of the poem on the Internet. Listen and check if your sequence is correct.

C Discussion

Work in groups to discuss these questions.

(1) Which of the following things is the *dead man* concerned about? Which stanza(s) are about them? And how are they different between when he was alive and after he died?

Things the dead man is concerned about now	Which stanza(s)	What did he do with them before his death	How are they now after his death
Harness bells			
Horses			
Farming			
Playground			
Young people			
Sweetheart			
Family			
Parents			
Furniture			
Friend			
Football			

(2) Compare the results of the comparison in the above table between what remains the same, and what has changed before and after the death of the questioner. What message do they convey to the reader?

(3) Study the arrangement of the stanzas. Can we change their sequence? Why?

(4) What tone can you detect in the answerer when he answers the questions?

D Role-play

Work in pairs to develop the poem into conversational English so that you can talk to your partner in an appropriate form of question and answer. Act out the dialog as if two people talk on telephone.

Proverb

Love is like coke: something you get as the product of making something else.

PART 2 Reading and Language Activities

Text — Someone Waiting

▶ Pre-reading tasks **Discuss the following questions.**

1. How would you feel when you, after a long journey, see somebody waiting for you at the railway station?

2. Did anyone see you off when you left for college? How were you feeling then? Which of the following words apply to your case?

nervous	upset	happy	joyful
delightful	sad	mixed	apprehensive

3. Do you know the following flight-related terms?

flight number	airline	check-in	boarding gate	pickup
boarding pass	arrival	departure	security check	

▶ Read the text

I am sitting at an airport watching people in the final moments before their loved ones arrive or depart. They are pacing, nervous, looking at one another, touching and not touching. The emotion is charged.

A woman, speaking Spanish, is running in circles trying to gather family members together for a good-bye. Her voice is high-pitched. When the final moment comes before boarding, she wraps her arms around her son, giving him a powerful embrace that should protect him until he returns.

A grandmother and grandson stand at the rail where I am waiting; the people who are supposed to pick them up are late. Two ladies, next to them but unrelated, look up and down the corridor as if scanning an open sea. A mother holds a baby as she kisses her husband. Tears dampen her cheeks. The moment is charged.

At Gate 13, the arrivals are just coming in. "I see her. There she is." Just as poignant, the arrivals fold into the mix of people as if they have been the missing ingredient. There are tears and smiles, pure delight ringing in the laughter of seeing someone who has been gone.

I sit, glancing at my book, waiting for my turn to leave, alone because the ones I love have a different schedule from mine, and the one I am going to see, a daughter, is at the other end of my journey.

I think of other departures and arrivals. I recall seeing my daughter, the daughter I am now going to visit, coming down that narrow corridor with her backpack slung on one shoulder, her overstuffed carry-on cradled in her arms, her headphones making her oblivious to the stream of people flowing along with her. She was in her first year at university coming home for a holiday in November — the first time since August. I wrapped myself around her as if she had been lost to me.

Today my flight is two hours late. The book I am reading is not as interesting as the people leaving and coming, coming and leaving. A little boy about five is meeting his grandfather for the first time. He looks up and up at the face of a man who is not that tall, except to a child. Joy shines down and up, and I am wondering how one would capture this moment in words or on film.

When my flight is finally called, I gather my books and carry-on. Since there is no one to see me off, I do not look back to see where I have come from. Instead, I think of my husband at work wondering if I have left yet, and my daughter at the other end wondering the same thing.

As I head toward the plane, I find myself remembering yet another arrival and departure. When I was a newlywed, my 91-year-old grandfather died. We had been very close, and one evening, returning from his funeral, I arrived at the airport crying. My husband of only a year was waiting at the gate to take me in his arms. Because of my tears, everyone was looking at us, but I didn't care. Somehow the emotion I felt seemed not at all out of place for the airport.

Life needs to be this important all the time. I wish all the people who went on a journey could come back to find someone waiting for them. I also wish they could leave with someone to see them off. I think of my grandfather and realize that if dying is like this, a passage, then I am unafraid.

Comprehension work

A Read the text again and discuss the following questions.

1. At an airport, how do people usually behave in the final moments before their loved ones arrive or depart?

2. How is the Spanish-speaking woman expressing her emotion before her son leaves?

3. What happens to the waiting people and the arrivals when they finally meet at the airport?

4. What does the narrator remember as she heads toward the plane?

5. What conclusion does the narrator draw from her observation? Do you agree with her? Why?

B Activity

Make Observations

The narrator notices many small things happening at the airport as expressions of love between people. Have you also noticed acts of love in your life? Make a comparison between Chinese and American styles of showing love in places of meeting and departure.

2 ▶ **Language work**

A Fill in the following blanks with the words or phrases from the text.

1. The emotion at an airport is always _____. People are coming and leaving, leaving and coming. They _____ the _____ board of arrival and departure. They constantly _____ at their watches.

2. For the leaving passengers, their loved ones give them a powerful _____ before _____. Women kiss their husbands and children. Tears _____ their cheeks. Men are _____ nervously. You may wonder how one would _____ this _____ moment in words or on film.

3. Those who come to _____ somebody are waiting at the rail and looking up and down the _____. Occasionally, two people, though _____, would talk to each other for a while.

4. At one gate, the arrivals are just coming in. They are _____ the waiting crowds with their _____.

5. Once people find someone they are waiting for, they wave to them and shout with _____ voice. Those arrivals _____ themselves around the waiting people and quickly _____ the mix of crowds. You hear the laughter of pure _____.

B Rewrite the following sentences with the expressions in the box.

oblivious to	head toward	pick up	be supposed to
out of place	glance at	take ... in the arms	

1. When the rescue operation began, military troops immediately moved in the direction of the earthquake site.

_____

2. Since her children are still in kindergarten, the mother must first go there and take them home.

_____

3. It's after three o'clock now. But she expected to meet me here at two o'clock.

_____

4. When his friends talk about modern paintings, Mr. Smith keeps silent and feels awkward and uncomfortable because he knows little about the subject.

_____

5. The boy with his eyes fixed on the screen didn't notice the knock at the door.

_____

6. When the mother learned the news that her son had failed in the university entrance examination, she put her arms around him encouraging him to try again.

_____

7. When waiting for the train in the subway, many passengers buy a newspaper and have a quick look at the headlines.

_____

C Word study.

a. **Give the meanings of the following words or expressions used in the text. You may use an English-English Dictionary. Then give a sentence to illustrate their meanings and usage.**

1. in circle(s)

_____

2. as if

_____

3. next to

_____

4. in words

_____

5. wonder (how / what / if)

_____

b. **Each of the following clues has an example sentence. Use the prompts to produce other sentences with the same pattern as the example.**

1. Prompt: woman / run / in circles / try to

Example: A woman is running in circles trying to gather family members together for a good-bye.

a. students / sit / in circles / talk

b. flowers / grow / in circles / wave

c. child / run / in circles / play

2. Prompt: two ladies / next to / look up and down / as if

Example: Two ladies, next to them but unrelated, look up and down the corridor as if scanning an open sea.

a. man in a sport jacket / standing next to / ask / as if

b. girl / next to the window / jump / as if

c. old wooden bridge / next to the temple / stand / as if

3. Prompt: wonder / capture / in words

Example: I was wondering how one could capture this moment in words or on film.

a. wonder / record / solemn moment / in words

b. wonder / express / emotion / in words

c. wonder / describe / view / in words

PART 3 Extended Activities

1 Dictation

2 Read more

The Important Things

For years the children whimpered and tugged. "Tell us, tell us."

You promised to tell the children some other time, later, when they were old enough.

Now the children stand eye to eye with you and show you their teeth. "Tell us."

"Tell you what?" you ask.

"Tell us The Important Things."

You tell your children there are seven continents and five oceans.

You tell your children the little you know about sex. Your children tell you there are better words for what you choose to call — The Married Embrace.

You tell your children to be true to themselves. They say they are true to themselves. You tell them they're lying, you always know when they're lying. They tell you you're crazy. You tell them to mind their manners. They think you mean it as a joke; they laugh.

There are tears in your eyes. You tell the children the dawn will follow the dark, the tide will come in, the grass will be renewed, every dog will have its day. You tell them the story of *The Little Soldier* whose right arm, which he sacrificed while fighting for a noble cause, grew back again.

You say that if there were no Evil we wouldn't have the satisfaction of choosing the Good. And if there were no pain, you say, we'd never know our greatest joy, relief from pain.

Notes

1. whimpered: whined, asked in a plaintive way, as small children do
2. tugged: pulled insistently (at clothing, for example)
3. mind their manners: (colloquial) be more polite
4. relief from pain: an end to pain
5. fudge cake with chocolate frosting: an American treat for children, a cake coated with a sugary chocolate topping
6. The Married Embrace: a euphemism for sexual behavior
7. *The Little Soldier*: a traditional story whose moral is that good behavior will be rewarded
8. The dawn will follow the dark: a well-known saying that implies that life will go on
9. Every dog will have its day: a well-known saying which implies that everyone gets something out of life

You offer to bake a cake for the children, a fudge cake with chocolate frosting, their favorite.

"Tell us," say the children.

You say to your children, "I am going to die."

"When?"

"Someday."

"Oh."

You tell your children that they, too, are going to die. They already knew it.

You can't think of anything else to tell the children. You say you're sorry. You are sorry. But the children have had enough of your excuses.

"A promise is a promise," say the children.

They'll give you one more chance to tell them of your own accord. If you don't, they'll have to resort to torture.

A True / False / Not Mentioned (NM).

1. You promise to tell the children something important immediately when they ask you earnestly.
2. Children know more about sex than you can tell them.
3. Children are more likely to ask difficult questions than their parents.
4. You try to give children conventional wisdom in the form of wise sayings, but they laugh at them.
5. You offer to bake a cake for the children so that they can be satisfied and will not pester you with questions.
6. The children don't feel shocked when you tell them something about death.
7. You feel sorry because you can't find anything else to satisfy the children's needs.
8. The story indicates a truth that parents usually cannot cope with the growing desire of children to know more about life.

B Topics for discussion.

1. What do you think are the important things in one's life?
2. Comment on the last sentence: If you don't, they'll have to resort to torture.
3. What do the children really want to know? Give your opinion.

3 Grammar work

Correct the mistakes in the following sentences.

1. John and Mary are friends and the both like classical music.
2. No one of us think so.
3. Tom was nowhere to be found. His teacher looked everywhere for him but in vain.
4. Every one of the children in the United States is to receive some form of education.
5. Every sex has its own physical characteristics.
6. Each my aunts gave me gifts for Christmas.
7. The house he lives in is half mile away.
8. The police have each reason to believe that he is the murderer.

4 Word formation

Fill in the following blanks with derivatives of the words in the box.

| hard | light | ash | sweet | strength |
| earth | dark | sharp | soft | fast |

1. Robin _____ the stick at both ends with a knife.
2. The streets were _____ by big trees on the two sides.

3. John looks terribly sick, pale and _____.

4. These were the _____ pots discovered in that tomb.

5. "I'm sorry to hear the sad news about your mother." Emma said in a _____ voice.

6. He stressed the need to _____ the ties between the two countries.

7. After the rain stops, the sky _____ up a little.

8. The tea was _____ with honey.

9. The glue dries very fast and _____ in an hour.

10. When he took his seat on the plane, he _____ the seat belt as instructed by the airline attendant.

> *-en*: a suffix normally used to form a transitive verb from an adjective, e.g. harden, meaning to make hard or harder. The suffix *-en* can also be used to form adjectives from nouns, e.g. golden, meaning having the color of gold.

5 ▷ Vocabulary work

The milestones of life

Use an English-English dictionary to group the following words and phrases into three categories — birth, marriage and death.

bouquet	funeral	get engaged	grave
pregnant	godmother	have a baby	nappy
grief	bury	widower	maternity leave
wedding	christening	bridegroom	pram
mourners	honeymoon	get divorced	wreath
coffin	sympathy	exchange rings	bride

Birth	Marriage	Death

6 ▷ Translation

Put the following sentences into English.

1. 我不喜欢上火车站给人送行。**see ... off**

2. 公司星期一晚上为你举办告别晚会，七点半有车到旅馆来接你。**pick up**

3. 她太激动了，情不自禁地热烈拥抱我。**give ... an embrace**

4. 我从未摆脱局外人的感觉。**out of place**

5. 她环视房间，想看看谁在那儿。**glance**

6. 他的大鞋子看起来像只小船。**look like**

7. 你应该把鸡蛋搅进面粉，而不是反过来做。**fold into**

 Writing

A What are the important things in life?
   Finish the following sentences and add one more.

As far as I'm concerned, an interesting job
_____.

As far as I'm concerned, an interesting job is most important. I can't bear to do a boring job.

a. Personally, one of the most important things in life is _____.

b. It seems to me that it's important to _____.

c. In my opinion, what's important is _____.

d. From my point of view, the important thing is _____.

e. I believe that _____.

B Write about your feelings the first time you left home for college, or about how parents accompany their children to college.

Cultural Information

 Read the passage below, and then complete the task of cultural study.

Pub Culture

Public houses (pubs) are an important part of British culture. People (pub-goers) go there not only for drinks (alcoholic or soft drinks), but also for socialization. In many ways, the pubs are the most popular places for people to gather to exchange information, meet friends, talk about topics of common interest, play games (such as darts, billiards, the pool, or the snooker which is getting increasingly popular in recent years) or just kill time. It is said that pubs are one of the domestic tranquilizers ever invented — "the revolution starts at closing time!" is the popular cry.

A typical British pub interior is characterized by three objects: a bar, a traditional fireplace, and a slot machine (a gamble machine where the customer plays by inserting coins). Customers (who are often called locals because of their regular or frequent visits) usually go to a pub nearby and don't change for many years. Some customers who have a particular taste in meeting people will go to special theme pubs, such as a football fan pub, a gay pub, or a pop music pub.

Pubs have well-defined rules for opening and closing times as dictated by local laws. Disregard for these rules will result in revoking of the licenses.

 Cultural Study Task

English pubs even go down to the nursery rhyme *Pop Goes the Weasel!* Carry out an internet study to find out the origin of the song. "Up and down the City Road / In and out The Eagle / That's the way the money goes / Pop goes the weasel." Where is the City Road? What is The Eagle? and What does weasel mean?

(Note: It is highly likely that you will find variant versions of this song in different English speaking countries.)

Unit

6

Football

Introduction

In this unit, you will learn to use English for

▸ Showing concern and breaking bad news softly
▸ Talking about the history of football
▸ Talking about British and Chinese modern football systems

PART 1 Communicative Activities

1 ▷ Interactive listening and speaking

A Listening

In this recording, you will hear the talk between a football coach Mr. Harris and one of his players called Sam. They are going to play an important match. Before you listen,

predict what they would talk about.

a) Arrangement of the equipment

b) Division of bonus

c) Selection of players

d) Arrangement of positions in the match

Now, listen and check your prediction.

B Interpretation

Listen to the recording for several times, and explain the differences between the literal meanings and their implications of the conversation in this context. The first one has been done as an example.

The sentences from the conversation	Literal meanings	Their implications
Sam, I want to talk with you about this match on Saturday.	Ice-breaking, Showing intention to talk with Sam.	I have some bad news for you. I wish that you were ready and reasonable.
But I was thinking ... you know, the game is a bit distance this time ... I'm concerned about your family ... may be difficult for you to ...		
There's no problem here ... distance is no problem for me ...		
London team ... strong, ... have lost last three games ... under ... pressure, ... thinking of trying some new blood		
Let's be frank, Sam. We know ... as hard as anyone on the team, but both of you fouled a lot recently ... if you can be dropped this time, we may give both of you another chance sometime ...		
Oh, no. ... let me put it straight, Mr. Harris! ... You either have me play ... or lose the game, to be frank with you.		
Well, decision has been made ... hope you understand ... I'm sorry.		

C Discussion and speaking.

In this recording, Mr. Harris broke bad news very gently to Sam. How would he speak when he has good news to break? Let's say he is going to talk to Martin, a substitute player. It's been decided that he's going to replace Sam in this game. Now, work with your partner to role-play a dialog between them.

2 ▶ Pragmatic implications

It is well known that language can express more than what words or sentences literally mean. The China Customs at the international airports of big cities like Beijing, Shanghai, or Guangzhou usually post big banners for welcoming the inbound passengers. Read the following list of candidates for English banners and choose the best one for them. Then discuss your choice in your group. You should reach agreement finally. If you are not happy with any of them, you may suggest your own version.

Candidates for the banner above the Customs Counter	My choice and the reasons
1) Welcome to China. One world One Dream!	
2) Warmly welcome!	
3) Welcome to China!	
4) Hi! Step in to China.	
5) Welcome! No smoking anywhere.	
6) Warmly welcome! No plastic bags are allowed.	
7) Warmly welcome you! Please get your passports ready.	
8) Welcome! China is one of the greatest countries in the world.	
9) Welcome to China. No joking with the immigration officers.	
10) Hi. No littering or spitting.	
11) Welcome! Friendship! Cooperation! Harmony!	
12) Enjoy your stay in China!	

● **Proverb**

Cooperation • Honor • Fairness •
High moral and physical standards

PART 2 Reading and Language Activities

Text Football

▶ Pre-reading tasks **Discuss the following question.**

What is the origin of modern football?

1 ▶ Jigsaw reading

Jigsaw reading means reading cooperatively with your classmates. Please follow the following steps.

(1) Join a group of five students.

(2) Read one section out of the following five sections of (A), (B), (C), (D), and (E). Take notes while reading. Don't read any of other people's sections.

(3) Tell other four group members about what you have learned from your section. (You may use your note if you can't remember the details.)

(4) Listen to other four people in turn. Work out the correct sequence and a summary of the article.

(A) By the end of the 18th century, however, the game was in real danger of dying out in Western Europe. Curiously enough, it was the English "public" school that saved it from extinction. The rich young men at these schools (which were in fact private rather than public) had nowhere to hunt, fish, ride or otherwise use up their energies; all they could do outside school hours was to kick a ball in the schools' open spaces. They played the game that they had often seen played on village greens, the game that kings had banned. Gradually each school began to evolve its own special style and rules.

(B) In 1863, the Football Association (FA) approved a game that outlawed carrying and kept the ball at men's feet. The game still had a long way to go, however, before it would be the football watched by millions around the world on television during the World Cup. Whole teams would rush back and forward on the field with the ball kept close at their feet; there were no passes or long kicks, and some of the rules used in those days were still nearer rugby than football. By the early 1870s, however, the fast, exciting, and open game of modern Association football was beginning to appear. The goal became standard, with a hard crossbar instead of a long piece of tape, and the goalkeeper was the only person permitted to use hands to play. In the process, football changed irrevocably from a gentleman's weekend exercise to the greatest spectator sport in the history of human race.

(C) In the Middle Ages, some kind of "football" was popular in Italy, France, England, and Scotland, but it was such a dangerous game that kings actually banned it, and for 300 years it suffered greatly from official disapproval. Nevertheless, in 1613, the King of England permitted himself to be entertained in an English village with "music and a football match", and, a few years later, the English dictator Oliver Cromwell played football when he was at university.

(D) By the time of Queen Victoria, enthusiastic schoolboys were writing out rules for what had once been no more than violent military or village fun. They also took the game with them to the universities. But more rules were needed so that people who had played very different kinds of football at school could play together successfully at university. This was how the Football Association came into being. One public school, however, refused to co-operate. Its delegates objected to the new universal game. This school — Rugby — left the new association to play its own game with its own oval-shaped ball that could be carried as well as kicked. In this way, football and rugby were born and went their separate ways.

(E) Football is a very old game. The ancient Romans, Chinese, and Mexicans all played games where men kicked a ball. For the Romans it was a war game, in which two teams of soldiers would use whatever force was necessary to get the ball across either of two defended lines. The Roman Empire has long since vanished, but the violent pastime of the armies has continued — and can still be quite violent.

You may write your results in the space below.

⭐ The sequence is: _____

⭐ The summary:

2 ▶ Language work

A Fill out the following blanks with the words or phrases from the text.

1. Football was saved from _____ thanks to public schoolboys by the end of the 18th century.

2. The Roman Empire _____ around AD 395. The Romans are remembered for being brave but cruel fighting men, who liked to watch men and men or animals and men fighting to death as a form of entertainment. So it was not strange for the Roman soldiers to play football as a _____ war game.

3. King James I (1566 — 1625) was King of England from 1603, and King James VI of Scotland (from 1567). He was the son of Mary, Queen of Scots. He was the first king to _____ himself to be entertained with the football game.

4. Hunting, fishing, riding, and shooting used to be normal sports for wealthy people. When the public school boys _____ _____ to do these activities, they had to play "football" in the schools' _____ _____ to _____ _____ their energies. But at that time, the game was _____ _____ _____ violent military or village fun.

5. Do you know how the game "rugby" _____ _____ _____? When the FA wanted to make the game a _____ one, one of the schools called "Rugby School" _____ _____ this idea. It wanted to play the game in its own way. Thus, rugby and football _____ _____ _____ _____. And since then the FA has become the ruling body only for football. Today, the FA controls both the amateur and the professional game and arranges the FA Cup in Britain. But rugby _____ into two forms: rugby union and rugby league. The former is played by professional players and the latter by amateurs.

B Rewrite the following sentences with the expressions in the box.

| write out | die out | object to | a long way to go |
| save ... from | use up | come into being | go their different / separate ways |

1. For religious reasons, they strongly opposed this new law.

   _____

2. The doctor went into his office to sign a birth certificate.

   _____

3. When did the universe start to exist?

   _____

4. The traditional grocer's shops are becoming less and less common now that there are so many supermarkets.

   _____

5. With a long handle on the brush, you will not have to bend down to clean the floor.

   _____

6. Mother told me not to finish all the flour in the bag.

   _____

7. Housing and sanitary conditions have improved greatly in recent years. But there is still a lot to be improved.

   _____

8. They used to love each other very much. But now, after the divorce, they are like strangers, never having anything to do with each other.

   _____

C Word study.

a. **Give the meanings of the following words or expressions used in the text. You may use an English-English Dictionary. Then give a sentence to illustrate their meanings and usage.**

1. long since

   _____

2. in danger of

   _____

3. no more than

   _____

4. outlaw

   _____

5. in the process

   _____

6. irrevocably

   _____

b. **Each of the following clues has an example sentence. Use the prompts to produce other sentences with the same pattern as the example.**

1. Prompt: Roman Empire / long since / vanish / but pastime of the armies

   Example: The Roman Empire has long since vanished. But the violent pastime of the armies has continued.

   a. truth / long since / become apparent / but

   b. deadline / long since / pass / but application letters

   c. long since / forget / she / say / the quarrel / but she

2. Prompt: game / in danger of / die out

   Example: By the end of the 18th century, the game was in real danger of dying out in Western Europe.

   a. panda / in danger of / die out

   b. many people / in danger of / lose / jobs

   c. bridge / in danger of / wash away in the flood

3. Prompt: football game / no more than / military or village fun

   Example: By the time of Queen Victoria, the football game had become no more than violent military or village fun.

   a. they / live / room / no more than / 15 square meters

   b. she / write / long report / no more than / trivial matter

   c. kid / praise / no more than / small progress

4. Prompt: Football Association / approve / game / outlaw

   Example: In 1863, the Football Association approved a game that outlawed carrying the ball in hand.

    a. the United Nations / pass / a bill / outlaw / use of poison gas in wars

    b. nobody / object to / proposal / outlaw / the selling of cigarettes to adolescents

    c. congress / resolution / outlaw / radical organization

5. Prompt: in the process / football / change / irrevocably / from ... to

Example: In the process, football changed irrevocably from a gentleman's weekend exercise to the greatest spectator sport in the history of human race.

    a. in the process / human civilization / develop / irrevocably / from matriarchal / to patriarchal society

    b. in the process / the planned economy / change / irrevocably / market economy

    c. in the process / fit / replace / unfit / irrevocably / survive in the world

PART 3 Extended Activities

1 Dictation

2 Read more

The World Cup

    One of the first things that people studying English learn is that the game they call football is called soccer in North America. Soccer has been popular for more than 100 years, and today it is probably the most popular sport in the world.

    Every four years, teams from all over the world compete in the famous World Cup. The Cup is a series of games in which teams from many countries play to see which is the best. By one estimate, almost one billion people watched the 1982 championship game on television. People in Asia had to get up in the middle of the night to see Italy beat West Germany on TV in a game played in Spain.

The World Cup began in Montevideo, Uruguay, in 1930. At the time, it did not seem like a true world competition since only 13 teams decided to play, and eight of them were from South America. The team from Uruguay won.

In 1934 and 1938, the Cup was held in Europe. More than 30 teams played in each of these competitions, and Italy won both of them. The larger number of teams meant that some rules had to be changed. There were too many teams playing, so they had to have elimination matches first. Some of the games were played in countries other than the host country. This system is still used today, and only the 24 teams left after elimination actually compete for the Cup.

There were no World Cup championships in 1942 or 1946 because of World War II. The cup itself was hidden during the war. This beautiful cup is about ten inches high and has the shape of Nike, the Greek goddess of victory, on it. It is named for a person who helped organize the World Cup, Jules Rimet.

When Cup play started again in 1950, there was little enthusiasm. It was like 1930 all over again: Only 13 teams competed, the games were in Brazil, and Uruguay won. But the worldwide interest in soccer came back during the next four years. By the time West Germany won in Switzerland in 1954, millions of people wanted to go to the matches.

In 1958, when the games were held in Sweden, interest was once again very high. Fifty-three teams wanted to compete. Many elimination matches were held in different parts of the world to get the number of teams down, and only the last 16 teams went to Sweden. This was the first time that the world saw Pelé. His team, from Brazil, won the Cup for the first time that year, and Pelé became the greatest soccer player of all time.

In the past 30 years, soccer has become the sport of the world. Each World Cup is more successful than the last. Since 1966, probably one-quarter of the world has listened to or watched the championship game.

> **Note**
>
> only the 24 teams left: The number of the teams for the final tournament is actually not fixed. For example, there were 32 teams participating in the 2010's World Cup Tournament in South Africa.

True / False / Not Mentioned (NM).

1. Football is called soccer in Britain.
2. The World Cup final is always played in the middle of the night.
3. Britain had objection to the idea of playing football at the World Cup at the beginning.
4. The rules of having elimination matches did not exist until 1934.
5. World War II prevented the World Cup from taking place.
6. The cup was seized by the Germans as a trophy during the Second World War.
7. People had little interest in competing for the Cup in 1950.
8. Pelé became the greatest soccer player of all time because his team won the Cup in 1958.

Grammar work

Correct the mistakes in the following sentences.

1. The apple trees in our new garden look like not more than a branch. They are too young to bear fruit.
2. We met Jane but no Elizabeth.
3. The FA developed football and standardized.
4. You may speak both English and Chinese at the meeting.
5. These boys not only play football very well, but play rugby.
6. James is not a good player as his father.
7. Either Tom and Jim has your pen.

 Word formation

Not all "-or" or "-er" suffixes are used for persons. Look at the following list of words and figure out what each of them refers to a thing, a person or both.

1. a cooker _____
2. a typewriter _____
3. a ticket-holder _____
4. a record player _____
5. a cleaner _____
6. a smoker _____
7. a drinker _____
8. a supervisor _____

> *-er* is often used for people in sports, e.g., footballer, swimmer, wind-surfer, high-jumper, cricketer, golfer, etc. The word *player* is often necessary, e.g., tennis player, basketball player, volleyball player; we can also say football player, cricket player. Some words must be learnt separately, e.g., canoeist, cyclist, mountaineer, gymnast, and motorist.

 Vocabulary work

Playing sports

Fill in the following blanks with the words and expressions in the word box.

take up	beat	by	record
defeat	score	give up	hold

1. Our team lost _____ three points.
2. She broke the Olympic _____ last year.
3. He _____ the record of 100 meters free-style.

87

4. The Shanghai club team _____ Guangzhou 4–2 yesterday.

5. The team has never been _____.

6. How many goals did you _____ in the match?

7. I think I'll _____ tennis in the new year and _____ badminton.

6 ▶ Translation

Put the following sentences into English.

1. 他认为他们之间的婚姻只不过是个交易而已。**no more than**

2. 他把身上的钱花了个精光。**use up**

3. 这位年轻人从水里把你女儿救了出来。**save ... from**

4. 她实在无处可去，于是就呆在家里看看旧书。**nowhere to**

5. "我能成为像杰夫 (Geoff) 那样的好球员吗？" "也许可能，不过离那一天还早着呢。"
   a long way to go

6. 他那份工作看样子干不长了。**in danger of**

7. 工厂雇佣童工的情况在许多国家已绝迹了。**die out**

7 ▶ Writing

A Work on your own.

Respond to the following statements by agreeing or disagreeing. Then develop the statement with one or two additional sentences.

Example:

The earliest football was played by the Romans.

 Respond: Yes, it was. At that time, it was played by the Roman soldiers as a war game.

   Or: Yes, it was. But it was not only played by the ancient Romans, but also by ancient Chinese and Mexicans.

   Or: No, it wasn't. The author is wrong. Some experts say that the origin of football is still unknown.

1. Football game used to be quite dangerous.

   _____

2. Football used to be a very expensive game. Only the rich could afford it.

   _____

3. The public schools banned football in the 17th century.

   _____

4. The modern version of football started from 1863 when the Football Association outlawed carrying the ball in hands.

   _____

5. In the game called "rugby," the players are permitted to handle the ball with their hands.

_____

B   The Chinese Football Association.

(Tip: If you don't know how to express yourself in English, the following section of Cultural Information may help.)

How much do you know about the Chinese football organization? If you don't know it, ask your partner or classmates. There must be somebody in your class who knows the relative information.

You may use the following questions to elicit the necessary information.

1. Who controls professional football games in China?
2. How many divisions are there for professional games?
3. How many teams are there in each division?
4. What should a team do if it wants to move to a higher division?
5. When will a team be forced to move to a lower division?

C ultural Information

 Read the passage below, and then complete the task of cultural study.

Football

Football ("soccer" in American English) is a very popular sport in Britain, played between August and May (the football season). Many people, especially men, support a particular team and may go to watch the games that their team plays. Professional football is controlled by two organizations, the Football League and the Football Association (the FA). In England and Wales, there are 93 teams in the League, organized into four divisions:

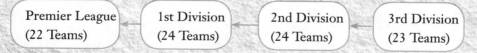

Premier League (22 Teams) ← 1st Division (24 Teams) ← 2nd Division (24 Teams) ← 3rd Division (23 Teams)

In Scotland, there are 38 teams in the League, organized into three divisions:

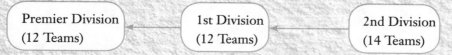

Premier Division (12 Teams) ← 1st Division (12 Teams) ← 2nd Division (14 Teams)

Teams play regularly in their league or division according to a fixed program. At the end of the season the team in the Premier League (or the Premier Division in Scotland) with the most points is the League Champion. This competition is called the League Championship.

The other important competition is the FA CUP, often just called the CUP. This is open to all amateur football teams that belong to the FA as well as the 93 professional teams. The teams play against each other in a knockout competition which starts in August and ends in May. The two teams left in the competition play in the FA CUP Final at Wembley Stadium in London. This is a very important national sporting occasion, watched by millions of people on television.

Unit

7

The English Countryside

Introduction

In this unit, you will learn to use English for

▶ Talking about rural views of Britain

▶ Talking about one's preference of living in the city or in the countryside

▶ Making an itinerary for a tour

PART 1 Communicative Activities

1 Interactive listening and speaking

A Listening

In this recording, you will hear a celebrity talking about ideas of living in the city or in

the countryside. Listen, take notes, and complete the following task.

In his talk, he mentioned five advantages of living in the city. What are they? Why does he think so? (The first advantage is given as an example.)

No.	Advantages	Why
1	convenience	
2		
3		
4		
5		

The celebrity implies or openly admits there are at least three disadvantages of living in the city. What are they? Work with your partner to write them out in the table below.

No.	Disadvantages	Why do you think so?
1		
2		
3		

B Interview

Work with your partner to design a series of interview questions (at least three) for the advantages and disadvantages of living in the countryside. Then interview the people from other groups. Write the results in the table below. And report the results to the class.

Interview questions	Interviewee's replies
Q1:	
Q2:	
Q3:	
Conclusion:	

2 ▷ Tourist picks

Suppose one of your teachers in the school wants to visit England for a tour. But they don't speak English. They'd like you to make some recommendations before they go. Now, listen to an audio clip about Yorkshire Dales in UK, and then select at least three reasons for recommending this place. Because some of the reasons listed below are not correct according to the video, you have to eliminate the incorrect ones first.

Your picks:	Why do you choose them?
(1) The Yorkshire Dales are one of the best loved areas in Scotland.	
(2) People all over Britain, Europe, and indeed the world often return to visit this place.	
(3) Yorkshire Dales are featured by dramatic beauty of limestone scenery cut out by acid rain through over 6 000 years.	
(4) There are over thousand miles of caves, underground passage ways, and caverns in the dales.	
(5) The Yorkshire Dales are a favorite place of potholing, and caving.	
(6) The Pennines, the central part of the mountain, have been one of the famous attractions for over two centuries.	
(7) The beauty of the dales reflects a rare balance between man and nature.	
(8) On top of the mountain range are bare, brown and moraine summits in contrast to the beauty in the lowlands.	
(9) The big nascent wildness is due to thousand years of clear felling of original forests for sheep grazing, and lead-mining.	
(10) Vast grass moors are artificially created and maintained for a recreational activity.	
(11) Farm houses in the valleys today are outlined by trees of the scattered woodlands.	
(12) The hamlets, harm houses are organically built of the local materials so that they look as if they grow out of the rock itself.	
(13) Many rivers and villages in the region take their names from dales.	
(14) Yorkshire Dales are one of 40 national specially protected parks in Britain.	
(15) The dales today are world famous for its richness in geology, natural history, and its importance of archeology, history, and culture.	
(16) Summer is the best season to enjoy the beauty of the scenery.	
(17) The dales are famous for world famous sheep-raising, crafts-making, dry- stone-wallers, sweet-makers, and landscape artists.	

Notes

1 pennines: low-rising mountain range
2 waller: the mason who builds walls

Proverb

Grass is always greener on the other side of the fence.

PART 2 Reading and Language Activities

Text   The English Countryside

▶ Pre-reading tasks   **Complete the following tasks.**

Study the following words and phrases; select the ones that can be applied to describe the views in your place, and imagine which of them can be used to describe the English countryside.

bush	rivers	meadow	lawn	coast	beach
footpath	brook	stream	valley	lowland	upland
corn field	bay	estuary	broad	fields	hills
landscape	rural	pasture	rice-paddy	cultivated land	
the wilderness	cliffs				

▶ Read the text

Most Englishmen, if only because of the natural formation of their island, are essentially more at home in the lowlands than on the heights. The popular idea of an English village is of one in a valley, where it can be overlooked from the hills, clustered about its ancient church; and similarly, the general conception of a farm in this country is of a more or less commodious homestead in a valley, sheltered by ample trees, with broad fields like open hands stretched out to receive the sun, and a river flowing not far away. There is always a river not far away in England; and although judged by Continental standards, our rivers may for the most part be small and insignificant, they are perhaps more intimately known for that. Certainly they are not the kind about which national songs are composed, as in the case of the Rhine or the Danube or the Volga; but at least they are the kind in which a boy can bathe and in which (even today) a farm-hand can tickle an occasional trout. They permit of such homely occupations as the gathering of watercress or the growing of osiers for basket weaving; and although the mill-wheels they once turned are silent now and weed-clogged, men still lean over the weirs on summer evenings and watch the swallows cross the clear water under the bridges. Such rivers,

94

insignificant as they may be, influence the lives of those who live near them in the most subtle and sensuous way.

For some time I lived in a cottage on the western edge of the Cotswolds. In front of my garden a meadow — itself a garden of cowslips in spring and a haunt of bee-orchises that fell with the swaths of grass in summer — dipped down to the Severn Valley. Standing at my door, I could see across the lowland orchards and pastures to the Malverns on the one hand and to the Welsh Mountains on the other. Those far blue ridges might be hidden by mist or cloud from time to time; but seldom was there a day when I could not clearly follow the course of the river down to its wide muddy estuary. Year in, year out, the Severn was part of my view; it was even part of my consciousness.

Notes

1 the Rhine: the longest river in West Europe. (莱茵河)

2 the Danube: a long and important European river. (多瑙河)

3 the Volga: a river in Russia, the longest in Europe. (伏尔加河) The Rhine, the Danube and the Volga are all the subjects of well-known songs.

4 cowslip: 黄花九轮草

5 bee-orchis: 对叶兰 (产于欧洲，花呈蜂形)

6 the Severn: a large river in the west of England. (塞文河)

7 the Malverns: a range of hills in the west of England. (莫尔文山)

8 the Welsh Mountains: the mountains in Wales

9 the Cotswolds: a range of hills in west-central England, sometimes called the "Heart of England". The area has been designated as the Cotswold Area of Outstanding Natural Beauty. (科兹沃尔兹)

1 Comprehension work

A Read the text again and discuss the following questions.

1. Where do the majority of English people prefer to live?

2. What are the attractions of an English village?

3. What are the differences in rivers between England and other European countries?

4. What does the writer mean when he says "the Severn was part of my view; it was even part of my consciousness"?

B Activity

Work in pairs to find out the characteristics of the English countryside.

Aspects	Characteristics
Location	
Homestead	
Local activities on the river	
Mill wheels	

2 Language work

A Fill in the blanks with the words from the text.

1. The Rhine and the Danube are the two most important rivers in Europe. Well known for the charm and beauty in the summer, these rivers have become the _____ of many famous songs. The Rhine is more developed than the Danube, and carries more traffic following the _____ of the river. Both rivers provide _____ water for people of the areas.

2. The Malvern hills are situated in the west of England and _____ _____ to the south. On the hills you may_____ a lot of villages on the _____.

3. An English village is usually in a _____. In the center of the village stands a church _____ by houses and shops. Besides farming, the villagers may also be engaged in various homely _____.

4. An English farmer's _____ may differ in size, but it generally includes broad fields, an orchard, a garden, and a nice cottage _____ by trees.

5. The village pub is a place for the _____ and the local people to relax and chat after a day's work while the small river is a _____ for boys in summer.

6. The early years in the countryside have _____ my life in such a _____ way that they are embedded in my memory and have become part of my _____.

B Rewrite the following sentences with the words and expressions in the box.

permit of	be at home	sensuous	commodious
homely	insignificant	subtle	for the most part

1. When we lived in the country, we had a house with plenty of space.

   _____

2. Each individual's contribution to the fund seemed of little importance or value, but the total sum was very large indeed.

   _____

3. Many women in the countryside still carry on such simple and plain crafts as making jams and weaving baskets.

_____

4. I could not fully understand the lecture, because the speaker made a number of distinctions which were difficult to perceive or describe.

_____

5. A poet often has the ability to convey to his readers what he feels through his senses.

_____

6. When the birds were set free, they flew out of the cage and looked very comfortable in the trees.

_____

7. The rain forest in this tropic zone is generally dark and wet.

_____

8. The new software allows the computer to process data faster.

_____

C Word study.

a. **Give the meanings of the following words or expressions used in the text. You may use an English-English Dictionary. Then give a sentence to illustrate their meanings and usage.**

1. essentially

_____

2. more or less

_____

3. judged by

_____

4. in the case of

_____

5. on the one hand

_____

6. from time to time

_____

b. **Each of the following clues has an example sentence. Use the prompts to produce other sentences with the same pattern as the example.**

1. Prompt: Englishmen / essentially / at home / lowlands / heights
   Example: Most Englishmen are essentially more at home in the lowlands than on the heights.

   a. she / was born / US / essentially / more / a Chinese / than

97

b. Richard / essentially / soft / caring / though / look tough

c. John / essentially / a scholar / than / a politician

2. Prompt: conception / farm / more or less / commodious homestead

Example: The general conception of a farm in the country is of a more or less commodious homestead in a valley.

a. accident / she / become / more or less / handicapped / lose job

b. new student / more or less / familiar / subject / join in the discussion

c. children / mountain village / grow / more or less / in freedom

3. Prompt: judged by / Continental standards / our river / small / insignificant

Example: Judged by Continental standards, our rivers may for the most part be small and insignificant.

a. judged by / national standards / "Great Hotel" / only small inn

b. judged by / modern moral standards / Songjiang / reconciliation / government / sensible

c. judged by / Chinese standards / these rivers / only small creeks

4. Prompt: they / not / the kind / national songs / composed / as in the case of

Example: Certainly they are not the kind about which national songs are composed, as in the case of the Rhine or the Danube or the Volga.

a. Scientific advance / side effects / as in the case of / discovery / nuclear radioactivity

b. big rivers / origins / human civilization / as in the case of / the Yellow River and the Nile

c. many discoveries / in dreams / as in the case of / sewing machine

5. Prompt: stand / I / see / lowland orchards and pastures to / on the one hand / on the other

Example: Standing at my door, I could see across the lowland orchards and pastures to the Malverns on the one hand and to the Welsh mountains on the other.

a. walk down / road / we / see / contrasting views / on the one hand / on the other

b. look out / you / see / mountain / on the one hand / river / on the other

c. go through / students' writing / teacher / discover / creative / on the one hand / poor skills / on the other

6. Prompt: ridge / hide / mist or cloud / from time to time

Example: Those far blue ridges might be hidden by mist or cloud from time to time.

a. nobody / would like / lecture / interrupt / from time to time

b. we / ask / direction / from time to time

c. white sails / obscured / cloud and mist / from time to time

PART **3** Extended Activities

1 Dictation

2 Read more

Village Life

"Oh, you're so lucky living in Bath, it's such a wonderful, lovely, historic place," people say enthusiastically, and all you can think of is the awful parking, the tourist crowding, the expensive shops, the narrow-minded council, and the terrible traffic ...

Luckily I don't live in Bath but nearly ten miles away in a village called Limpley Stoke in the Avon Valley. It seems to be normal in the countryside these days for professional people who work in the town to prefer to live in the villages; this makes the housing so expensive that the villagers and agricultural workers have to live in the cheaper accommodations in town, with the result that the farmers commute out to the farm and everyone else commutes in. Certainly, there's nobody in the village who could be called an old-style villager. The people nearest to me include a pilot, an accountant, a British Rail manager, a retired French teacher ... not a farm worker among them. But I don't think there is anything wrong with that — it's just that the nature of villages is changing and there is still quite a strong sense of community here. A lot of this sense of community comes from the Post Office, which is a center for all the gossip and information. I find out what is going on while I am there, pretending to control my two-year-old son. He enjoys anything he can touch at the lowest level of the shop, which consists mainly of an enormous rack of cards saying "Congratulations on your 9th Birthday" and a collecting tin for the "Save The Children" charity which he always picks up and tries to run away with. My feeling is that if my son took the money collected for the children it would go directly where it was needed but they don't see it like that.

Working at home, I tend to wander round the village at times when other people are at the office, which has given me a reputation for being incredibly lazy or unbelievably rich, but I still don't get enough time to look after the garden we bought. My wife had a good idea for the first year. "Let's just leave it and see what comes up." We did.

There were some nice plants among the weeds. She had a good idea for the second year as well. "Why don't we leave it and see if it all comes up again?" We did, and that is why we need to hire a full-time gardener this year.

Roman Bath

Pictured here is the natural hot spring originally attracted the Romans, who founded the city of Bath in England. The Romans discovered a medicinal value in the springs and excavated the baths, which are now famous landmarks.

A Choose the best answer to each of the following questions.

1. What is the author's attitude about Bath?

   a. It is a wonderful place to live in.

   b. It has far too many disadvantages.

   c. He feels fortunate to live there.

2. The people who live in the village _____.

   a. tend to work on the farms

   b. are mostly professionals who work in the town

   c. are unable to afford houses in the town

3. It would appear from the text that the post office _____.

   a. sells a wide range of cards

   b. is where most of the charity work is organized

   c. is a place where villagers can talk to each other

4. The author has a reputation for being rich or lazy because he _____.
   a. seems to be free when other people are working
   b. spends a lot of time shopping with his son
   c. likes to walk around the village
5. The garden is not in very good condition because _____.
   a. the author is too lazy to look after it
   b. the author has not been able to find a gardener
   c. nobody has worked on it for two years

B Topics for discussion.
   1. What is the nature of a true village?
   2. What causes the change of the village?
   3. Is the change for the better or worse in your opinion?

3 Grammar work

Correct the mistakes in the following sentences.

1. I want to buy a thriller because I love to be excited and thrilling in reading.
2. Everybody is pleased to the results.
3. The old lady was really shocking at the terrible mess in the house.
4. It is quite annoyed to interrupt one's talk.
5. Local people are disturbing at the news that a wild animal is still at large.
6. Are you satisfactory with the design of the new product?
7. Shakespeare is known with his famous plays.
8. The speaker was bored — you could see it on the faces of the audience.
9. Researchers were disappointing at the result of the test.
10. Her remarks were rather confused.

4 Word formation

Fill in the following blanks with derivatives of the words in brackets.

1. "How did you like the film?"
    " It was _____ (fascinate)."
2. Despite dangers and difficulties, the soldiers were _____ (determine) to win the battle.
3. It's true that living in the city may be _____ (bore), but I think you'll be _____ (amuse) if you are observant enough to look into its culture.
4. She was _____ (embarrass) when they kept _____ (tell) her how clever she was.
5. We were very _____ (worry) when the children didn't come home.

> **Adjectives ending in "-ing" or "-ed"**
>
> Many adjectives can be formed by adding "-*ing*" or "-*ed*" to a verb. Usually, adjectives with the "-*ing*" suffix describe the effect that something or someone has on your feelings, or on the feelings of people in general. For example, if you talk about "a surprising number," you mean that the number surprises you. However, the adjectives with the "-*ed*" suffix often describe people's feelings. They have the same form as the past participle of a transitive verb and have a passive meaning. For example, "a frightened person" is a person who is frightened by something or someone.

 Vocabulary work

A Here are some useful adjectives for describing towns and the countryside. Sort them out and arrange them under the right heading. (Notice: Some of them can be listed under both.)

picturesque	historic	spacious	elegant	magnificent
lively	bustling	crowded	hilly	filthy
shabby	rustic	run-down	quiet	beautiful
packed	pastoral	rural	deserted	

Towns	The countryside

B Study the following words and phrases, put them into different groups.

Study more phrases that are often used to describe views and landscapes. Put these phrases into the following four categories.

> **Words and phrases**
>
> wonder at the heights of mountains, the mighty waves of the sea, the wide sweep of rivers, the cycle of the oceans, deserts, and the revolution of the stars, islands, disturbing, fearful, vast, nature conquered, virgin beauty of the wilderness, cut to shape, and almost "man-made", nature boxed-in like a domestic pet, the artificiality of city, garden, forests, and moorlands, views to delight / feast one's eyes / senses, silent, dark, cold, airless, full of unknowns, forests are the abode of beasts and bandits, foreign, appalling, the unholy wilderness, full of mischief and evil, a place of order and virtue, pleasant natural scenes

Aspects	Expressions and phrases that may be used in this category
Romantic aspects of the wilderness	
Wild, uncivilized aspects of nature	
Civilized aspects of nature	
Neutral aspects of nature / the wilderness	

6 ▷ Translation

Put the following sentences into English.

1. 她卧室有几扇可以眺望美丽湖景的大窗。**overlook**
2. 他瘫倒在扶手椅上，两腿向前伸着。**stretch out**
3. 那儿我实在住不下去了，我在那里度假时天天下雨。**day in and day out**
4. 仓库保持干燥非常重要，对于这些药物来说尤其是这样。**in the case of**
5. 这个村里的人多半温文尔雅，彬彬有礼。**for the most part**
6. 在我们这个地区，冬天往往很冷，夏天则温暖而干燥。**tend to**
7. 这个菜只有牛肉和蔬菜，做起来很简单。**consist of**

7 ▷ Writing

A Work on your own.

You have to be careful about the use of "the" with geographic names. The following table provides some rules.

Case	Use with "the"	Examples
Countries whose names contain one word	no	China, France
Countries whose names contain a common noun	yes	The US
Countries when limited by time	yes	The Spain of today
Individual mountains	no	Snowdon
Mountain chains	yes	The Himalayas
Islands	no	Sicily
Groups of islands	yes	The West Indies
Rivers	yes	The Volga

Oceans	yes	The Pacific
Seas	yes	The Mediterranean
Gulfs, bays and straits	yes	The Gulf of Mexico
		The Strait of Gibraltar
Lakes	no	Lake Erie

Describe your places

Use the following cues in the brackets to describe a place you are familiar with.

1. _____ (About a famous river)
2. _____ (The location of the river)
3. _____ (About a famous mountain / mountains)
4. _____ (Are there any famous cities or towns nearby?)
5. _____ (The importance of the river and the mountain(s))

B Compare a Chinese village with the English village you have read about in the text. Fill out the following table. (Write at least three points.)

The English village	The Chinese village
• in the lowlands rather than on the heights ... • homestead and its surroundings — overlooked from hills ... • clustering about the church, sheltered ... • influences of the rivers ...	

C ultural Information

Read the passage below, and then complete the task of cultural study.

The British Countryside

The British countryside is varied and in places very beautiful, especially in such regions as the West Country, the Lake District, the Yorkshire Dales, the mountains of Wales and Northern Ireland, and the Scottish Highlands. It comprises not just farmland but large areas of forest, moorland and upland. The overall charm of the countryside is enhanced by Britain's many rivers, streams, and canals, and by varied coastline, with its many bays and beaches. There is also plenty of wider country one can get to, and much of this is in National Parks and National Forest Parks. These are where the countryside and its animals are specially protected. All of this makes for a land where tourism is one of the major industries, and where a "country walk" is regarded as one of the chief recreational pleasures.

 Cultural Study Task

Use the information on the Internet to complete the task below.

Suppose you are given £500 to spend in a five-day-tour in the Cotswolds in England. Write your itinerary of the tour based on the information from the website: http://www.cotswolds.info/. Your international flights are covered already.

> You may follow this guideline:
> 1. What are your daily activities? How much would each of them cost? How much do you plan to spend?
> 2. How do you arrange your accommodation (room and board)? Where do you stay and eat? How much do you plan to spend?
> 3. How do you arrange your local transportation? How much do you plan to spend?

Unit

8

Beauty and Career

Introduction

In this unit, you will learn to use English for

- Talking about the meaning of "beauty" and "beautiful"
- Discussing the phenomenon of cosmetic surgery
- Talking about woman's participation in engineering

PART 1 Communicative Activities

1 Interactive listening and speaking

A Listening

What is your attitude towards cosmetic surgery? What is your definition of "beauty" and "beautiful"? In this recording, you will hear a radio talk show hostess Mary and her two guests, Sue, a former top model, now a businesswoman, and Elizabeth, a

writer and university lecturer talk about their different views on cosmetic surgery.

Preliminary listening

Read the following attitudes, and predict who might hold them. Listen and check your answers.

Speakers	Attitudes	Statements of attitudes to cosmetic surgery
Mary		Indifferent
		Interested
Sue		Supportive
		Opposing
Elizabeth		Neutral

Listening again

There are many facts mentioned in their talk show for, against, or just neutral about cosmetic surgery. Listen, and then put these facts into different categories as they are used in the talk show. Some facts are in fact acknowledged by both sides.

No.	Facts	For	Neutral	Against
1	Some people suffer from disorders and anorexia.			
2	People enjoy coming to spas.			
3	People have only one body to look after.			
4	Some European women used to have their ribs removed in order to look thin in the waist.			
5	It's up to everyone to decide what is right for him / her.			
6	Neck-stretching was a fashion in some parts of Burma.			
7	There is too much emphasis on the appearance these days.			
8	Thousands of women have breast implants, eye-lid operations, and face-lifts.			
9	People live on this earth only for a short while.			
10	Foot-binding was very common in the old China.			

11	Some women stretched their ear lobes or lips in order to look beautiful in Africa.			
12	People have freedom to choose what they want to do.			
13	Two beautiful people participate in this talk show.			
14	People feel they look like ten years younger when they leave spas.			
15	It is just a trend that keeps increasing.			
16	There are a lot of people who are unhappy because of their appearance.			
17	Women have to experience physical pain in order to look beautiful.			
18	People are often judged by their appearance.			

B Talk

Work in pairs to discuss the following questions:

1. Whose argument is more convincing to you? Who are in favor of it? Why?

2. Do you agree that the society is forcing women into the beauty salons, or spas?

C Activity

Suppose you were the program host / hostess. You have just finished the talk show on "beauty," on which your guests Sue Jaycee and Elizabeth Young presented their views. But one listener called in to say that she missed the program and asked if you could brief many of your listeners again on the discussion. Of course you don't want to disappoint your friendly listeners. So give them a brief account of the discussion, introducing both sides of the argument. You may use the following guidelines for the presentation.

Presentation Organizer

Who are the guests and what do they do?

What is Sue's view?

What is Elizabeth's view?

Your comment on this discussion.

---

2 Language work

A Fill in the following blanks with the words from the text.

Mary Has it always been in fashion for women to have thin waists, Elizabeth?

Elizabeth No, not always. But they enjoyed a (1) _____ popularity for centuries in Europe. Women used to wear wooden or metal corsets to give them thin waists.

Mary From a modern (2) _____, it sounds rather amusing. What a (3) _____ thing to do!

Elizabeth I'm afraid it wasn't very funny most of the time. The women had to (4) _____ a lot of pain. Sometimes the corsets damaged their internal organs, like the liver.

Mary But there is a (5) _____ here between the past practice and the (6) _____ ideas, isn't there? We still put a lot of (7) _____ on having a thin waist, don't we?

Elizabeth That's right. Some people even have (8) _____ (9) _____ to remove fat from their stomachs. The surgeon inserts a tube and sucks out the fat. It's a growing (10) _____, especially in America.

Mary Oh, it sounds (11) _____ to me. I could never have that done.

B Rewrite the following sentences with the expressions in the box.

happen to do something	ridiculous	keep on	go in for
no point in doing something	judge ... by	be up to	go to ... lengths

1. While living in the countryside, she developed a special interest in gardening.

   _____

2. Father spent a great deal of time and effort to give the old house a face-lift.

   _____

3. Since we have already settled the problem, it is meaningless to talk about it again.

   _____

4. It is the students' responsibility to decide their future careers.

   _____

5. The manager will view the project in terms of its net profit.

   _____

6. When he was thumping melons for a ripe one, the boy accidentally stepped into a rattler's mouth.

   _____

7. It is foolish and unreasonable, scientists have argued, to talk of computers as if they were human brains.

   _____

8. They continued walking for a while in silence.

   _____

● Proverb

Beauty is skin deep.

PART 2 Reading and Language Activities

Text — Media Madness

▶ Pre-reading tasks **Complete the following tasks.**

(1) Which of the following characters would you normally associate with women?

    a. Sensitive

    b. Careful

    c. Technically savvy

    d. Communicative

    e. Humorous

    f. Dexterous

(2) Match the words with pictures. (Write them in the correct brackets.)

Words:	a. (　　)	b. (　　)
push pin / thumbtack USB thumb drives CD-Drive		
hard drive cubicles cork board floppy disks	c. (　　) 	d. (　　)
	e. (　　) 	f. (　　)

g. ( )

Have you thought of a woman engineer's life? Karen has a story to share with us. Read her story and then complete the tasks.

▶ Read the text

Media Madness
A Story from a Woman Electronic Engineer
By Karen Panetta

I was cleaning out my office recently and came to a large floppy disk with holes punched in it from push pins. Why on earth would I keep such a thing? (1) _____ _____ It came from my first internship at the Fiber-electro Company.

I worked in the Information Systems department as a systems analyst. One of my responsibilities was designing custom database solutions for those individuals not skilled in using computers. (2) _____ That was until one day when two managers came storming into my office complaining that they had lost their data and the floppy disks I gave them no longer worked. I looked at one of the disks and noticed that it was full of holes made from a thumbtack.

I asked him, "Why are there holes in the disk?" The manager replied, "I had it pinned up on my cork board to make sure I didn't misplace the disk."

I tried not to laugh but recorded a mental note that I needed to update the user manual I created for my non-computer savvy users to tell them that punching holes into the disk was a no-no.

(3) _____ With a smile and look of confidence he replied, "I use a magnet to hold it up on the metal wall of my cubicle and I don't use any push pins!"

I thought I would choke trying not to laugh and waited for them to tell me this was all just a joke to evoke a reaction out of the poor naïve intern. I then gave a short tutorial on the manufacturing and operation of floppy disks and explained why magnets and poking holes in the media storage meant certain death for their data. (4) _____ _____.

As powerful as the digital age is, the loss of data through the transition to new forms of media storage makes me wonder how much valuable history and other defining characteristics of our civilization will be lost over time. (5) _____

_____ What we know comes from the few surviving parchments and records etched in stone. Data carved in stone seems to be the most fault tolerant form of media storage and can survive for thousands of years. What about our digital media? (6) _____ _____ What would someone in the far-off future discovering an ancient USB thumb drive, hard drive, or CD-ROM do with these ancient relics? They might do like my mother did and make a picture of a giant shiny fish using the disks that I have thrown out over the years.

You may be asking what brought on this morbid train of thought. (7) _____ I was trying to find a picture I took with a digital camera. I have hundreds of images with randomly assigned names provided by the camera. In the old days, I would print out my pictures and stuff them in an album.

Now everything is on the computer. What is worse is that I literally kill my computers within two years of purchase, such that I have gone through more hard drives in my lifetime than I have new pairs of shoes.

I even bought an NAS to use as a backup system just to store my pictures on so I wouldn't lose them. (8) _____ I always seem to lose something during the transition from one computer to another or to some newer current state of the art media storage.

(9) _____ I should make a necklace out of them by handing them off a rope like shark teeth, since I can't remember what's stored on the drives anyway. There isn't a search engine on the planet that can keep up with my huge quantities of disorganized media and data.

I finally gave up on retrieving the picture for which I was looking. (10) _____ _____ Then when I gave up all hope, my mother called me. I told her how I spent hours searching the computer for a specific picture, when she described with great detail the exact picture for which I was looking. I asked her how she knew and she said, "Because I'm looking at the eyeball of the fish I made out of those shiny circles you always throw out and one of them is labeled with that exact description. I also remembered that you told me that if I glued them, I would destroy the information on them, so I tacked them to the board using push pins in the hole in the middle to secure it in case you ever wanted them back."

I borrowed her fish's eye-ball and successfully retrieved my picture. At this time, I really don't need to etch my data in stone to have it survive. It appears that having it stored on a fish is sufficient.

Notes

1. Adapted from IEEE Women Engineering Magazine, Volume 4: no.1, pp.12-13, June 2010.

2. NAS: Network-Attached-Storage is a computer connected to a network that only provides file-based data storage services to other devices on the network. NAS units usually do not have a keyboard or display, and are controlled and configured over the network, often using a browser.

Comprehension tasks

A Put these sentences back into their correct positions in the article.

No.	Sentences	Positions
a	I have an arsenal of USB thumb drives.	
b	We wonder how the pyramids were built and know that there had to be some incredible engineers during those ancient times.	
c	I'll tell you.	
d	The second manager's floppy disk looked intact, so I asked him how and where he stored his disk.	
e	Like an ancient civilization, it was lost forever.	
f	I was returned to sainthood in their eyes when they discovered I kept a backup of everything.	
g	The users loved my software and thought I walked on water.	
h	This memento also had significance in my career.	
i	It doesn't matter.	
j	What would happen if power was lost and the knowledge of computers vanished forever?	

B Humor

The writer tries to be humorous in the article. Here are some quotes from the article; some of them are just told in "a matter of fact" tone, while others sound humorous. Discuss which of them are humorous, and why you think so.

a. Why on earth would I keep such a thing?

b. That was until when one day two managers came … no longer worked.

c. The manager replied, "I had it pinned up … I didn't misplace the disk."

d. I tried not to laugh … that punching holes into the disk was a no-no.

e. With a smile and look of confidence he replied, "I use … and I don't use any push pins!"

f. What is worse is that … my lifetime than I have new pairs of shoes.

g. Data carved in stone seems … survive for thousands of years.

h. I should make a necklace out of them … on the drives anyway.

i. At this time, I really don't need … It appears that having it stored on a fish is sufficient.

113

2 ▶ Language work

A Phrases in context.

Explain these words or phrases according to their context.

(1) storm into my office

(2) record a mental note

(3) non-computer savvy users

(4) a no-no

(5) give a short tutorial

(6) defining characteristics of our civilization

(7) the most fault tolerant form

(8) the morbid train of thought

(9) kill my computers within two years of purchase

(10) be returned to sainthood in their eyes

(11) walk on water

(12) some newer current state of the art media storage

(13) when she described ...

B Word study.

a. Give the meanings of the following words or expressions used in the text. You may use an English-English Dictionary. Then give a sentence to illustrate the meaning and usage.

1. go in for

   _____

2. no point in

   _____

3. the way I see it

   _____

4. free to do

   _____

5. remove

   _____

6. keep ... fit

   _____

b. Each of the following clues has an example sentence. Use the prompts to produce other sentences with the same pattern as the example.

1. Prompt: tribes / go in for / stretch / ear lobes

Example: In Africa, there were tribes which went in for stretching the ear lobes.

    a. slim and slender / young woman / go in for

    b. I / not like / people / go in for / wear odd clothes

    c. young people / in city / go in for / roller-skating

2. Prompt: I / not see / point in / look back at

Example: I don't see there is any real point in looking back at all these quaint old customs.

    a. I see / no point in / this kind of exercise

    b. no point in / persuade / him / because

    c. there / no point in / repair / broken bike

3. Prompt: the way I see it / you / short time

Example: Now, the way I see it, you're only on this earth for a short time.

    a. the way I see it / achievement tests / cancel

    b. the way I see it / cigarette / no good / human beings / cigarette factories / close

    c. the way I see it / rich countries / not be immune / economic crises of south-eastern Asia

4. Prompt: we / talk / people / free to choose

Example: We're talking here about people who are free to choose.

    a. university students / free to choose / job

    b. in old days / young people / not / free to marry

    c. you / free to choose / subjects at school?

5. Prompt: women / bottom ribs / remove / thin waist

Example: In Europe, some women had their bottom ribs removed so that they would have thin waists.

    a. I'd like / books / desk / remove / so that

    b. she / remove / her hand / his arm

    c. we / chairs and desks / remove / so that / enough room for party

6. Prompt: you / keep / yourself / fit

Example: You've got to keep yourself fit.

    a. we / exercise / keep ... fit

    b. she / work hard / keep ... fit

    c. middle-aged women / attend / aerobic classes / keep ... fit

PART 3 Extended Activities

1 Dictation

2 Read more

Women and Beauty

In almost every part of the world and in every age men have tried to limit the possibilities open to females by hindering their movement. The foot-binding of upper class Chinese girls and the Nigerian custom of weighing women's legs down with kilos of heavy wire are extreme examples. But all over the world similar methods have been used to make sure that once you have caught a woman she cannot run away, and even if she stays around she cannot keep up with you.

What seems odd is that all these apparatus have been seen as beautiful, not only by men but by women as well. Tiny feet, which seem to us a deformity, were passionately admired in China for centuries, and today most people in Western society see nothing ugly in the severely squeezed toes produced by modern footwear. The high-heeled, narrow-toed shoes that for most of these centuries have been an essential part of women's costume are considered attractive, partly because they make the legs look longer. They also make standing for any length of time painful, walking exhausting and running impossible. The way of walking produced by them is thought to be attractive perhaps because it guarantees that no woman wearing them can outrun a man who is chasing her. Worst of all, if they are worn continually from the teenage years on, they deform the muscles of the

Notes

1. Samantha and Sammy: Samantha is a name for female whereas Sammy is for male.
2. grapefruit: large, round fruit of a tropical or semitropical evergreen, having a yellow rind and juicy, but very acid pulp (西柚，葡萄柚)

feet and legs so that it becomes even more painful and difficult to walk in flat shoes.

Modern women's shoes are what keeps Samantha from running as fast as Sammy, literally as well as figuratively. As anyone who has worn them will agree, it is hard to concentrate on your job when your feet are killing you — especially if you are faint with hunger because you had only half a grapefruit and coffee for breakfast so as to stay a beautiful five kilos below your natural healthy weight. For a while in the sixties and seventies it was not necessary to be handicapped in this way unless you chose to be. During the last few years, however, women have begun wearing tight, high-heeled shoes again; and the most fashionable styles are those that give least support to the feet and make walking more difficult.

A Choose the best answer to each of the following questions.

1. Men have tried to limit possibilities for women by _____.
    a. making it difficult for women to move
    b. using heavy wire apparatus to catch women
    c. allowing only women from upper classes to move around freely
    d. insisting that women are inferior to men

2. What is odd about the customs concerning women's feet?
    a. Tiny feet are considered beautiful by most people in Western society.
    b. People accept that modern shoes are ugly.
    c. Apparatus which deforms women's feet is not admired by men.
    d. Unnaturally shaped feet have been — and are — appreciated.

3. Why, according to the author, are high-heeled, narrow-toed shoes thought to be attractive?
    a. They change the appearance of the legs.
    b. Women have been wearing them for the last 100 years.
    c. They are an essential part of women's clothing.
    d. They encourage men to chase women.

4. What was the situation in the sixties and seventies?
    a. People went on diets to lose weight more than they do now.
    b. Women began to wear shoes which squeezed their toes.
    c. People had almost no choice regarding shoes.
    d. Fashion allowed wearing comfortable shoes.

5. What is the opinion of the author, concerning modern women's shoes, in the text as a whole?
    a. They are not very comfortable but are nevertheless attractive.
    b. They lead to difficulties only after many years of wearing them.
    c. They are not necessarily beautiful and cause many difficulties.
    d. Their design has been influenced by Chinese and Nigerian customs.

B Topics for discussion.

If women want to make themselves prettier, what is the best way in your opinion? Why?

 3 ▶ **Grammar work**

Correct the mistakes in the following sentences.

1. It was too proud for her to apologize.
2. He lay wake all night, thinking about his new job.
3. The doctors are working very hard to keep the patient living.
4. The two sisters are remarkably like in appearance.
5. I wanted to be lonely for some time.
6. "Don't disturb the asleep dog!" Mother warned.
7. Isn't she a content woman to have a handsome husband plus a healthy, intelligent son?
8. The listener was keen hearing Sue's talk about her cosmetic surgery.
9. The telephone is surely to ring again!
10. John found out that Tom was a glad man.

4 ▶ **Word formation**

Fill in the following blanks with derivatives of the words in brackets.

1. Mary felt very _____ (sleep) since she had been working all night.
2. Although this is a _____ (danger) task, nobody shows any sign of fear.
3. It will be a nightmare to travel in such a _____ (wind) and _____ (rain) day in this _____ (mountain) zone.
4. I'm very _____ (envy) of your new job.
5. She found the joke rather _____ (fun).
6. She had a longing for some _____ (juice), red ripe tomatoes.

> *-y* is used to form adjectives with the following meanings:
> 1) full of or covered with — dirty hands (covered with dirt); 2) tending to — curly hair (hair that curls); 3) like or typical of — a cold wintry day (typical of winter).
> *-ous* is used to form adjectives with the meaning of "causing or having":
> dangerous (= full of danger); spacious (= with much space).

 5 ▶ **Vocabulary work**

Human senses

Our basic five senses are seeing, hearing, taste, touch and smell. The five basic verbs referring to the senses are usually followed by an adjective rather than an adverb. For example:

He **looks** dreadful.

The trip **sounds** marvellous.

The cake **tastes** good.

It **felt** strange.

The soup **smelt** delicious.

Make a sentence using any of these verbs — *look, sound, taste, touch* or *smell*, plus an adjective about the given situations.

Example: You see a film about Mount Tai.

The mountains look magnificent.

1. You come downstairs in the morning and smell fresh bread.

   _____

2. A friend has just had her hair cut.

   _____

3. You hear the record that is the top of the pops.

   _____

4. A friend, an excellent cook, tries a new recipe.

   _____

5. A friend asks how you feel today.

   _____

6. A little boy asks you to listen to his first attempts at the piano.

   _____

7. You see a friend of yours with a very worried look on his face.

   _____

8. Someone you are working with smells strongly of cigarettes.

   _____

6 ▷ Translation

Put the following sentences into English.

1. 我发现要跟上时装变化是困难的。**keep up with**
2. 他不太喜欢室外运动。**go in for**
3. 我的英语不好，翻译这首诗歌还不行。**be up to**
4. 人们通常以貌取人。**judge ... by**
5. 她看起来好像整夜没睡。**look as if**
6. 他决定不惜代价去实现他的雄心壮志。**go to great lengths**
7. 为了听得清楚些，他坐在前排。**so as to**

 **Writing**

A Work on your own.

Read the following quotations about "beauty." Comment on them in one or two sentences.

E.g. It is better to be beautiful than to be good. But ... it is better to be good than to be ugly.

Yes. It is human nature to want to be more beautiful. But that doesn't mean beauty is everything.

1. Beauty is only skin deep.

_____

2. Beauty is in the eye of the beholder.

_____

3. Don't judge a book by its cover.

_____

4. Remember that the most beautiful things in the world are the most useless: peacocks and lilies for instance.

_____

5. A thing of beauty is a joy forever: Its loveliness increases; it will never pass into nothingness.

_____

B Write a paragraph on the following topic.

Will you choose your boyfriend or girlfriend based on the first impression? Why or why not?

C ultural Information

Read the passage below, and then complete the task of cultural study.

Giving and Responding to Compliments

To compliment means to say something positive about someone for showing friendship and good will. In English, it is polite and very common to give compliments about the following situations.

1. A person's physical appearance:

   e.g.   You look wonderful.

   You're the prettiest girl I've ever seen.

2. A person's attributes and abilities:

   e.g.   I really enjoyed your speech.

   You did a good job.

   You write beautifully.

   Well done.

3. Clothing and possessions:

   e.g.   I like your tie.

   That's a beautiful ring.

   That color looks nice on you.

   Your stereo system sounds great.

4. Food:

   e.g.   That soup is delicious.

   That dish smells wonderful.

5. Environment:

   e.g.   This is a great apartment. It's so big.

   I like the view from your window.

It is also polite to make an appropriate response to a compliment to show that you accept the friendship and acknowledge the good will. The commonest way of response is to say "thanks". In addition, you can say something more to show you agree with the assessment. For example:

Mary: This is such a nice apartment. It's so sunny.

Linda: Thanks. I really enjoy living here.

Notice the differences between Chinese and Western cultures in responding to compliments. Chinese people tend to think that one should be modest when they are complimented. But in English it is polite to appreciate others' compliments. In many cases, therefore, it is inappropriate, for example, to say in English "I didn't do well" or "It's my duty" in responding to the compliment "Well done".

 Cultural Study Task

Try to ask native speakers from English speaking cultures on the following questions:

Do they think these topics are suitable for complimenting an adult?

a) One's silky skin

b) One's big eyes

c) One's make-up
d) One's social skills
e) One's eloquence

And then carry out a similar study among the Chinese. Write a report in about 500 words on the results of the comparative study.

Secret Messages to Ourselves

Introduction

In this unit, you will learn to use English for

▶ *Expressing intentions*
▶ *Talking about good / bad / cool inventions*
▶ *Talking about how inventions are made*

PART **1** Communicative Activities

 Interactive listening and speaking
A Listening

  In this recording you will hear one of the middle school students talking about his inventions in the school activities at the Show and Tell Session in his class. Listen, and fill in the gaps with proper names of the inventions.

Invention 5:
Name: _____
Major features: _____
Materials: _____
Invention 4:
Name: _____
Major features: _____
Materials: _____
Invention 3:
Name: _____
Major features: _____
Materials: _____
Invention 2:
Name: _____
Major features: _____
Materials: _____
Invention 1:
Name: _____
Major features: _____
Materials: _____

B Talk

Suppose we want you to select five inventions that we can't live without today. What would you choose from the following list? Make a list of them, and share your picks in the group to reach agreement. Then report to the class.

The inventions that we can't live without today	
tea bag	telephone
dental floss	antibiotics
beer	cell phone
instant noodles	guitar
thermos	fridge
iPad	toothpick
shampoo	automobile
press printing	gun powder
tissue paper	timepiece
air-conditioner	

C Discussion

Good, bad, or just cool

Here are some inventions that people have made in recent years. Discuss the question in small groups. Are they good, bad or just cool inventions?

Inventions and their major features / functions	Good, bad or just cool
Beer Launching Fridge It is able to launch a can of cool beer from the fridge to the person seated in the couch so that he doesn't need to stand up and walk over to open the fridge in order to fetch the beer. What he needs to do is to press the remote control, and the fridge will throw a can of beer in his direction.	
Smile Profile Software A company in Japan invented software to analyze its employee's smile every morning. It tells you whether your smile is cheerful enough. If you're not, you have to smile wider.	
Gas-mask Bras It is a pair of bras that can also be used as gas-masks when one meets a gas bomb attack. You can wear them every day, but in case a gas bomb attack happens, you can take them off, and wear them to protect you.	
Computer Essay Reader As there are too many essays to read, a university teacher invented computer software to read the essay by counting word frequency, or length of sentences, and even the total words you used in the essay. So the teacher doesn't need to mark your essays or write comments anymore because it is time-consuming. With this software, the job can be done by the computer.	

Touchless Video Game Control It is one of the video gaming programs with a special device that can sense the movements of the gamers' body. So gamers are able to get rid of the gaming sticks. They can control the game just by waving their arms or kicking their legs around.	
LED Light Bulb An LED light bulb is invented to replace the traditional light bulb. A 10 watts LED light bulb can be as bright as a normal 60 watts light bulb, but uses only one sixth of electricity.	
Energy Hub It's a little box with a screen on it. You can put it in your house where you normally put your thermometer. It keeps track of all your appliances, TV, lamps, fridge, computers etc. It can display real-time how much electricity is used by them, and how much it would cost you. If it costs too much, you can use this energy hub to keep your energy bill under control.	

 2 **More sentences**

There are many ways to show one's intention. Here are some of the sentences for this purpose. Read, and match them with proper functions.

Actual words spoken	Functions
a. I intend to go back to work in my own country after I finish my studies here. b. Next time I see John, I'm going to tell him exactly what I think of him. c. I'm planning to move to Beijing in a couple of months. d. I don't intend to stay in this job all my life. e. I have no intention of buying a flat in this part of town. f. I have no plans to change my job in the foreseeable future.	1. Say you don't want to buy a flat here. 2. Say you don't want to remain in your present job for the rest of your life. 3. Say you want to go back and work in your own country after you finish studying here. 4. Say you are making arrangements to go to live in Beijing in one or two months. 5. Say you will tell someone your opinion of him if you see him again. 6. Say you will not change your job in the not-too-distant future.

● Proverb

Necessity is the mother of invention.

PART 2 Reading and Language Activities

Text   Secret Messages to Ourselves

▶ Pre-reading tasks   **Discuss the following questions.**

1. What kind of dreams do you often have? And can you remember them afterwards?
2. Do you believe that dreams may have a special meaning or message to us?

▶ Read the text

Early one morning, more than a hundred years ago, an American inventor named Elias Howe finally fell asleep. He had been working all night on the design of a sewing machine but he had run into a very difficult problem: it seemed impossible to get the thread to run smoothly around the needle.

Despite his exhaustion, Howe slept badly. He tossed and turned. Then he had a nightmare. He dreamt that he had been captured by a tribe of terrible savages whose king threatened to kill and eat him unless he could build a perfect sewing machine. When he tried to do so, Howe ran into the same problem as before. The thread kept getting caught around the needle. The king flew into a rage and ordered his soldiers to kill Howe. They advanced towards him with their spears raised. But suddenly the inventor noticed something. There was a hole in the tip of each spear. The inventor awoke from the nightmare with a start, realizing that he had just found the solution to the problem. Instead of trying to get the thread to run around the needle, he should make it run through a small hole in the center of the needle. This was the simple idea that finally enabled Howe to design and build the first really practical sewing machine.

Elias Howe was far from being unique in finding the answer to his problem in this way. Thomas Edison, the inventor of the electric light bulb, said that his best ideas came to him in dreams. So did the great physicist, Albert Einstein. Charlotte Brontë also drew on her dreams in writing *Jane Eyre*. The composer, Igor Stravinsky, once said the only way he could solve his problems in musical composition was to "sleep on them".

To appreciate the value of dreams, you have to understand what happens when you are asleep. Even then, a part of your mind is still working. This unconscious, but still active part digests your experiences and goes to work on the problems you have had during the day. It stores all sorts of information and details which you may have forgotten or never have really noticed. It is only when you fall asleep that this part of the brain can send messages to the part you use when you are awake. However, the unconscious part expresses itself through its own logic and its own language. It uses strange images which are sometimes called "secret messages to ourselves".

 Comprehension work

A Read the text again and discuss the following questions.

1. What had Elias Howe been working on all night before he finally fell asleep?
2. Did he have a problem? What was it?
3. Why did Howe sleep badly despite his exhaustion?
4. What made him awake with a start?
5. What did Howe suddenly realize?
6. Was Howe unique in finding an answer to his problem in this way? Are there any other cases in history in which some people found the answers in their dreams?
7. What happens to your mind when you are asleep?
8. How does the unconscious part of the mind express itself?

B Cloze

> After years of unsuccessful (1) _____ to work out the sewing machine, Elias Howe decided to give up his dream to become a great inventor. Depressed, and overwhelmed with strain, he went to bed one night, (2) _____ that his goal was unattainable. It was then that he had a dream, a very odd (3) _____, in which he was abducted by a tribe of savages. Through a jungle, he was carried to the tribe's king. "You have 24 hours to create a sewing machine for me!" shouted the (4) _____ king. "If you fail to do so, you should be immediately struck to death by (5) _____." In this odd dream, Elias recalled all his failed (6) _____, and with frantic effort, he constructed from prototype to prototype, desperate to satisfy his captors. Again and again, his (7) _____ flopped. Soon the 24th hour arrived with his deadline (8) _____. "No working sewing machine for me?" asked the king, "then (9) _____ by spear", he ordered. The savages arrived to surround him with raised spears. Looking up at the spears, he noticed a long hole at the pointed heads, and they (10) _____ from the savages' hands towards his belly. Elias felt no fear, no pain, but a spark of (11) _____. He had realized that if he created a prototype with a needle threaded at (12) _____, rather than attempting to mimic the manual techniques, which involved the tail threaded needle he would at last achieve success. Soon after his awakening, he fulfilled his goal of (13) _____ a sewing machine.

Language work

A Fill in the following blanks with words or phrases from the text.

1. Igor Stravinsky, the great Russian-American _____, had such a _____ talent for music that he could _____ any tiny discord in a music performance.

2. In writing her novel *Jane Eyre*, Charlotte Brontë _____ _____ her personal experiences as a governess.

3. In his experiment, Thomas Edison _____ _____ a lot of difficulties, which almost drove him to despair and _____. But finally he found _____ to all those problems.

4. Sigmund Freud was very interested in interpreting dreams and their _____. He _____ _____ them for thirty years and found out that dreams could _____ and process the information we got during the day.

5. _____ his financial troubles, Mr. Wilson insisted that he would _____ the small shop in town.

6. _____ _____ employing a builder, the family repaired the house themselves, which _____ them to get much pleasure from "Do It Yourself."

7. The terrible earthquake, during which all his family members lost their lives, is a _____ to him.

8. The _____ of the new product will not win the manager's approval _____ it can bring profit to the firm.

B Rewrite the following sentences with the words and expressions in the box.

unconscious	threaten to do something	fly into a rage	appreciate
toss	with a start	savage	digest

1. The explosion of a bomb made such a noise at night that people nearby all awoke in fear and surprise.

   _____

2. When he realized that he had been cheated, the man became very angry.

   _____

3. The employees warned that they would go on strike if they could not get a pay raise.

   _____

4. Do you fully understand the importance of his suggestion?

   _____

5. The ship was rocking from side to side on the rough sea.

   _____

6. During a war, human beings sometimes behave like wild animals.

   _____

7. It took him quite a long time to comprehend what was said in the report.

_____

8. A car crashed into a lamppost. The driver who was badly injured lost consciousness and lay on the road.

_____

C Word study.

a. Give the meanings of the following words or expressions used in the text. You may use an English-English Dictionary. Then give a sentence to illustrate their meanings and usage.

1. capture

_____

2. find solution to

_____

3. enable ... to do

_____

4. be far from

_____

5. despite

_____

6. express oneself

_____

b. Each of the following clues has an example sentence. Use the prompts to produce other sentences with the same pattern as the example.

1. Prompt: he / dream / he / capture / tribe

   Example: He dreamt that he had been captured by a tribe of terrible savages.

   a. thief / intend / run away / capture / policeman

   b. soldier / try / rescue / woman / capture / hostage

   c. you / capture / this moving scene / in words?

2. Prompt: inventor / realize / he / find solution to

   Example: The inventor realized that he had just found the solution to the problem.

   a. think over / problem / he / find solution to

   b. countries / serious / find solution to / climate changes

   c. we / must / find solution to / technical problem

3. Prompt: idea / enable / Howe / design / build / sewing machine

   Example: This was the simple idea that finally enabled Howe to design and build the first practical sewing machine.

   a. academic background / enable him to / find

  b. communication facilities / enable people to / communicate

  c. good vocabulary / enable / one / speak / write / more effectively

4. Prompt: Elias Howe / be far from / unique in

Example: Elias Howe was far from being unique in finding the answer to his problem in this way.

  a. he / diligent / be far from / top student

  b. quality / product / be far from / perfect

  c. mother / be far from / please / your examination results

5. Prompt: despite / exhaustion / Howe

Example: Despite his exhaustion, Howe slept badly.

  a. despite / difference / they / close friends

  b. despite / lack / bombs / soldiers still

  c. despite / bad climate / expedition team / go on / research work / in Antarctic

6. Prompt: unconscious part / express itself / through

Example: The unconscious part expresses itself through its own logic and its own language.

  a. dumb people / express themselves / by

  b. you / free / express yourself / with him

  c. student / express herself / in good, clear English

PART 3 Extended Activities

1 Dictation

2 **Read more**

Softball is Born   By Harold Keith

Outside the windows of the Farragut Boat Club in Chicago one November afternoon in 1886, gray rain poured down in long, wind-slanted lines, melodiously pelting the roofs and docks. George Hancock, a member of the club who was kept indoors, was pacing up and down, impatiently waiting for the shower to cease. But it wasn't a shower, it was a steady downpour. Hancock was bored, so he looked around for something to help him pass the time.

He spied a broom sitting in a corner. He picked it up, looked at it for a moment, then grasped it by the end of its handle and idly swung it as though it were a baseball bat. Then he looked about him for something to hit and saw an old tan boxing glove lying on a locker.

George Hancock had an idea, an idea so absurd that he laughed aloud as he turned it over in his mind. Carrying the boxing glove and the broom, he summoned several of his companions who were as bored with the rain as he.

"Come on, fellows!" he called, "we're going to play a new game. We're going to play baseball right here in this room. This broom will be the bat and this boxing glove will be the ball. What do you say?"

The others were willing, so bases were marked off. Soon they had all plunged into the game, shouting and laughing with enjoyment and forgetting all about the rain outside.

Thus softball was born. But it was not called softball at first and it was not played outdoors, as

Notes

1. softball: a variant of baseball, played with a larger ball on a smaller field. The ball is about 12 in. (30 cm) in circumference, about 3 in. (8 cm) larger than a baseball. Rules vary in different areas and among different groups. Two teams of nine or ten players compete in games that usually last seven innings. Invented in Chicago in 1886, softball is especially popular as a recreational game.

2. wind-slanted: coming down in a slanting line because of the wind

3. pelting: beating or striking heavily and repeatedly

4. spied: noticed something, especially when it is not so obvious (Formal use)

5. locker: a small cupboard for keeping things in. Lockers are usually found in schools, factories, or sports buildings where people can leave their outdoor clothes and personal belongings while working or playing.

6. turn it over in one's mind: to think a lot about it

7. YMCA: the Young Men's Christian Association; an organization in many countries which provides places to stay and sports centers for young people, especially in large cities, and is also concerned with their spiritual well-being. Its counter organization for females is called YWCA (Young Women's Christian Association).

8. while away: to spend (time) idly or pleasantly

thousands of American boys (and girls) play it today. It first became an indoor game, usually played in gymnasiums, and was known as kitten ball, indoor baseball, pumpkin ball, recreation ball, twilight ball, army ball, and playground ball. Despite this wide variety of names, the game mushroomed so rapidly that the schools, YMCA's, and recreation centers couldn't find enough indoor space for playing: consequently, it was moved outdoors, as early as 1908.

Softball's greatest growth dates from the depression in the early 1930s, when thousands of people who were out of work found softball a great way to while away the time and so forget their troubles. It quickly became an ideal sport for baseball-minded youngsters and adults.

A True / False / Not Mentioned (NM).

1. George Hancock was a good baseball player.
2. George Hancock invented softball because he liked to invent new things.
3. The first game of softball was played on a rainy day.
4. It was not until 1908 that softball became an outdoor game.
5. Softball flourished in the early 1930s.
6. Softball brought a lot of employment opportunities to Americans in the early 1930s.
7. The playing time of softball is shorter than any other games.
8. Softball is only suitable for old people.

B Topics for discussion.

1. What made George Hancock invent softball?
2. Why did softball become so popular in America?
3. What kind of personality is most likely to enable one to make an invention?

3 Grammar work

Correct the mistakes in the following sentences.

1. I have read the first English novel is *Jane Eyre*.
2. As soon as she came into the classroom that she began to read English.
3. Countries their banking systems were not well-developed suffered greatly in the recent economic crises.
4. The snow is very soft that I can hardly walk on it.
5. She went to bed until she had finished her homework.
6. Mary is the most intelligent student who I have ever known.
7. The boy studies music plays the piano well.

4 **Word formation**

Fill in the following blanks with derivatives of the words in brackets.

1. Nobody knows who were the oldest _____ (inhabit) on this island.

2. She became a _____ (Buddha) when she migrated to the _____ (Buddha) country.

3. I've just asked the sales _____ (assist) where the household appliances department is.

4. After thirteen years of hard work, he is now a world-famous _____ (piano).

5. Although he is a _____ (Vietnam), he can speak fluent _____ (Korea).

6. As most of the _____ (interview) are very nervous in front of the _____ (interview), we try to make them feel as relaxed as possible.

7. The _____ (host) of today's program is a distinguished _____ (act), Miss Elizabeth Wood.

> The suffixes *-ist*, *-ian*, *-ese*, *-ee* and *-ant* are used to form nouns which refer to nationality, people doing particular work, or people of a special kind. For instance: physics — physicist; China — Chinese; inhabit — inhabitant; employ — employee and Australia — Australian.

5 **Vocabulary work**

Fill in the following blanks with suitable words.

awake, waking

1. What he has said sounds like a _____ dream.

2. I drink a lot of coffee to keep myself _____.

afloat, floating

3. He managed to stay _____ by holding on to the side of the boat.

4. We spent a lazy afternoon _____ along the river.

frightened, afraid

5. She was _____ that he might be upset if she told him about it.

6. The police succeeded in rescuing the _____ girl at last.

sleeping, asleep

7. I was so tired that I fell _____ during the lecture.

8. A _____ bag is a large thick bag for _____.

live, alive

9. We were walking along a path in the forest when we suddenly saw a real _____ bear.

10. The city center comes _____ on Friday and Saturday evenings.

alone, lone

11. Entering the competition as the _____ outsider does not worry him in the least.

12. He likes being _____ in the house.

Translation

Put the following sentences into English.

1. 新的教育体制使大学生能够在学习的同时获得工作经验。**enable**
2. 作家必须利用他的想象力和生活体验写作。**draw on**
3. 这家公司一开始显得很有希望，但不久便负债累累。**run into**
4. "那份名单你写好了吗？" "还没有，我正在写呢。" **work on**
5. 尽管他们年龄差别很大，却成了好朋友。**despite**
6. 除非他更努力，否则他是通不过考试的。**unless**
7. 他为这个难题思考了整整一个星期后，最终解决了它。**turn over in one's mind**

 Writing

Comment on the following ideas about future inventions.

 animal language

I hope that someone can invent an animal language in the not-too-distant future.
With this linguistic invention, we would be able to communicate with dogs, cats and even birds.

Or I don't think this is possible. Animals don't have a well developed brain necessary for processing a complicated language system.

1. amphibious vehicles (flying and land cruising)
2. energy from water
3. medicine to cure cancers
4. computerized teacher
5. government system (the whole world becomes one family)
6. speedy vehicle (much faster than light)

C ultural Information

Read the passage below, and then complete the task of cultural study.

Archimedes and Eureka

Archimedes (287 – 212 B.C) was a Greek mathematician and inventor who established the rules for measuring density. He is believed to have discovered these rules while in his bath, and to have jumped out of his bath and run through the streets without clothes on shouting "Eureka! Eureka!" (I have found it! I have found it!) It means that he had found out how to measure the volume of an irregular solid and thereby determine the purity of a gold object. Today, the word eureka is frequently found in modern English, used to express triumph upon finding a solution or making a discovery.

 Cultural Study Task

How much do you know about Archimedes? What other sayings do you know about him? Who has said "Give me a place to stand on, and I will move the earth"?

Visit the website: http://en.wikipedia.org/wiki/Archimedes, and write a report in 500 words about his life, work, and famous sayings.

The Life Story of an Ancient Chinese Poet

Introduction

In this unit, you will learn to use English for

▶ Talking about classic poems and poets of the Tang Dynasty in China
▶ Interpreting the article about the Chinese poet Li Bai
▶ Critiquing literary works such as a poem

PART 1 Communicative Activities

1 ▶ Interactive listening and speaking

Listening

 In this recording, you will hear a professor of Chinese literature talking about three Chinese poems and poets in Tang Dynasty. He then gives a quiz after his lecture. First, go

over his quiz below, and then listen and complete the task.

Do you understand these terms? Translate them into Chinese.
- The imperial examination
- The doctor of the imperial college
- Court
- Daoism

Listen, take notes, and complete the quiz.

Quiz for Chinese Literature
Poems and Poets in the Tang Dynasty

Story 1
Poet's life story
Select correct points based on the lecture.
   a) He was famous for wealth and high ranking post at the imperial court.
   b) He was famous for his power of imagination, and love for drinking.
   c) He was a great scholar who was selected through the imperial examination.
   d) He abandoned the official post because he disdained authority and corruption.
   e) He loved life of nature more than the polished ways of living.
   f) He died a poetic death as legend goes.

The poet is:

a) Su Dongpo	b) Wang Wei	c) Li Bai
d) Du Fu	e) Li She	f) Han Hong

Questions about the poem

Green Mountains
Why do I live among the green mountains?
I laugh and answer not, my soul is serene;
It dwells in another heaven and earth belonging to no man.
The peach-trees are in flowers, and the water flows on.

● In this Q & A style poem, the **question** is:
   a) What do you see in the green mountains?
   b) How do flowers flow in the stream among the mountains?
   c) What kind of world are the green mountains like?
   d) What are the reasons that you want to live in the mountains?
   e) How can you make a living just on the peach-blossom and water from the stream in the mountains?

● And the **answer** is likely to be (there are more than one possible choices):
  a) I can't find an answer to your question.
  b) I don't want to answer your question.
  c) Who cares of this worldly idea?
  d) Don't bother my heart which is free of care.
  e) My ideal world is the one with flowers flowing down the stream.
  f) No man would question such a beautiful world in the mountain.

Story 2
Poet's life story
Select correct points based on the lecture.
  a) The poet met robbery on his journey to Jiu Jiang City.
  b) The gang leader asked the poet to choose between writing a poem for him or being killed.
  c) The robber thought that the poem is worth more than what money is worth.
  d) The poet and poem moved the gang leader so he stopped the crime, and left many gifts for the poet.
  e) The poet was saved by his clever servant.
  f) The poet treated the gang leader as a friend, and hoped to see him again in the future.
  g) The poet and his poem changed the gang leader into a good person.
  h) The poet and the robber met 50 years later in Guang Dong Province.
  i) The gang leader was grateful both for the poem and the poet.

The poet is:
  a) Su Dongpo   b) Wang Wei   c) Li Bai
  d) Du Fu   e) Li She   f) Han Hong

Questions about the poem
  Midnight Guests at Overnight Stay at Jing Lan Sha
  The evening rain is pouring. Travelling on the river to the village,
  Heroes from the green forest heard of it, and came to visit me.
  "No need to avoid me if we meet again in the future.
  Half of the people in the world are gentlemen."

● Who says "No need to avoid me if we meet again in the future. Half of the people in the world are gentlemen"? Which of the following understanding is more reasonable? Why?
  a) The poet narrator   b) the gang leader
  c) the servant   d) The poet

● Which of the following interpretations could be reasonable?
  a) Among the people here, half of us are gentlemen and half of us not.

139

b) Every human being is a complex combination of good and evil character.

c) People are changeable between being good and bad.

d) You may be a good person in some other time although you're a robber now.

e) In this world, good people and bad people are just fifty percent to fifty percent.

f) You're a great poet now, a good person, but you may become a bad person. Who knows?

g) We're gangsters, but we are good people sometimes. So there's no need to fear us.

h) If you treat us well, we are good people. But we are not if we're mistreated.

Story 3
Poet's life story

Select correct points based on the lecture.

a) Han Shi Jie means a day on which people are not allowed to make a fire for cooking.

b) Han Shi Jie seems to be in the thick of spring.

c) The poet failed many times in the Imperial Examination.

d) He wrote the poem *The Day of No Fire* in order to get a post in the imperial court.

e) The emperor did not like the poem although he appreciated the poet.

f) The poet was eventually selected by the emperor, and appointed a post in the government.

g) After his appointment, he wrote the poem to help the emperor.

h) The poet wrote the poem because he wanted to wipe out social inequalities.

The poet is:

a) Su Dongpo	b) Wang Wei	c) Li Bai
d) Du Fu	e) Li She	f) Han Hong

Questions about the poem

The Day of No Fire

The spring flowers are abloom about in every corner of the city,
On The Day of No Fire, an eastern wind bends willows in the imperial garden,
At dusk candles are passed out in the Han palace,
Their thin smoke swims into homes of five lords.

● Which of the following interpretations are reasonable? If you are not satisfied with any of them, interpret the poem in your own words.

a) The city was decorated by flowers on that day.

b) The wind was so strong that trees could not even stand properly.

c) The candles passed out were very old because they were handed down from Han Dynasty.

d) There are only five lords favored by the emperor.

e) Families of those other than the five lords were allowed to make a fire.

2 ▶ Story time

Turn the three poems into different genres of literary work: a narrative, a drama, and a conversation.

1) Turn *Green Mountains* into an interview between a journalist and the poet.
2) Turn *Midnight Guests at Overnight Stay at Jing Lan Sha* into a drama.
3) Turn *The Day of No Fire* into a narrative.

Draft your story in the space:

● Proverb

A person should claim recognition only for things that are not dependent upon others or not claim it at all.

PART 2 Reading and Language Activities

Text   A Life Story of a Chinese Poet   By Will Duran

▶ Pre-reading tasks **Discuss the following questions.**

1. How much do you know about Chinese poet Li Bai?
2. What else would you like to know?

▶ Read the story below, and answer the questions.

One day, at the height of his reign, the Chinese emperor Ming Huang received ambassadors from Korea, who brought to him important messages in a dialect which none of his ministers could understand. "What!" exclaimed the emperor, "among so many magistrates, so many scholars and warriors, cannot there be found a single one who knows enough to relieve us of vexation in this affair? If in three days no one is able to decipher this letter, every one of your appointments shall be suspended." For a day the ministers consulted and fretted, fearing for their offices and their heads, then Minister He Zhizhang approached the throne and said: "Your subject presumes to announce to your Majesty that there is a poet of great merit called Li at his house, who is perfectly acquainted with more than one science; command him to read this letter, for there is nothing of which he is not capable."

The emperor ordered Li to present himself at court immediately, but Li refused to come — saying that he could not possibly be worthy of the task, since his essay had been rejected by the mandarins at the last examination. The emperor soothed him by conferring upon him the title and robes of a doctor of the first rank. Li came, found his examiners among the ministers, forced them to take off his boots, and then translated the documents, which announced that Korea proposed to make war for the recovery of its freedom. Having read the message, he dictated a learned and terrifying answer, which the emperor signed, almost believing He, that Li was an angel descended from heaven. The Koreans sent tribute and apologies, and the emperor gave part of the tribute to Li. Li gave it to the innkeeper, for he loved wine.

Li Taibai, "the Keats of China", had discovered the world in AD701. "For twenty springs," he lived "among the clouds, loving leisure and enamored of the hills." He grew in health and strength, and became practiced in the ways of love.

> Wine of the grapes,
> Goblets of gold —
> And a pretty maid of Wu.
> She comes on pony-back; she is fifteen;
> Blue-painted eyebrows —
> Shoes of pink brocade —
> Inarticulate speech —
> But she sings bewitchingly well.
> So, feasting at the table
> Inlaid with tortoise shell,
> She gets drunk in my lap.
> Ah, child, what caresses
> Behind lily-embroidered curtains!
> And then the aftermath:
> Fair one, when you were here, I filled the house with flowers.
> Fair one, now you are gone, only an empty couch is left.
> On the couch the embroidered quilt is rolled up; I cannot sleep.
> It is three years since you went. The perfume you left behind haunts me still.
> The perfume strays about me forever; but where are you, Beloved?
> I sigh — the yellow leaves fall from the branch.
> I weep — the dew twinkles white on the green mosses.

He married, but made so little gold that his wife abandoned him, taking the children with her. Li Bai consoled himself with the grape and traveled from city to city, earning crumbs of bread with sheaves of song. Everybody loved him, for he spoke with the same pride and friendliness to both paupers and kings. At the capital the emperor befriended him, but could not command him. Says his fellow poet Du Fu:

As for Li Bai, give him a jugful,

He will write one hundred poems.

He dozes in a wine-shop

On a city street of Chang'an;

And though his Sovereign calls,

He will not board the Imperial barge.

"Please your Majesty," says he,

"I am a god of wine."

He accepted the philosophy of Liu Ling, who desired to be followed always by two servants, one with inexhaustible wine, the other with a spade to bury him wherever he might fall, for, said Liu, "the affairs of this world are no more than duck-weed in the river." So they soon seemed to be so to Li, for when Ming Huang lost his throne for love, the poet lost a patron, and fled from Chang'an to wander again over the countryside.

Why do I live among the green mountains?

I laugh and answer not, my soul is serene;

It dwells in another heaven and earth belonging to no man.

The peach-trees are in flower, and the water flows on.

His last years were bitter, for he had never stopped to make money, and in the chaos of revolution and war he found no emperor to keep him from that starvation which is the natural reward of poetry. In the end, after imprisonment, condemnation to death, pardon, and every experiment in suffering, he found his way to his childhood home, only to die three years afterward. Legend, unsatisfied with a common end for so extraordinary a soul, told how he was drowned in a river while attempting to embrace the water's reflection of the moon.

Shall we have one more of his songs?

My ship is built of spice-wood and has a rudder of mulan;

Musicians sit at the two ends with jeweled bamboo flutes and pipes of gold.

What a pleasure it is, with a cask of sweet wine and singing girls beside me,

To drift on the water hither and thither with the waves!

I am happier than the fairy of the air, who rode on his yellow crane,

And free as the merman who followed the sea-gulls aimlessly.

Now with the strokes of my inspired pen I shake the Five Mountains.

My poem is done, I laugh, and my delight is vaster than the sea.

Oh, deathless poetry! The songs of Chu'ping are ever glorious as the sun and moon.

While the palaces and towers of the Chu kings have vanished from hills.

Notes

1 The excerpt is adapted from *The Greatest Minds and Ideas of All Time* by Will Durant (1885 – 1981) who was awarded the Pulitzer prize (1968), and the Medal of Freedom (1977). Durant was best known for his critically acclaimed 11 volume *The Story of Civilization* (the later volumes written in conjunction with his wife, Ariel). He was famous for many of his books which brought knowledge out of the ivory towers of academia into the lives of millions of laypeople. The title of this passage is added by the of the authors of this textbook.

2 He Zhizhang: (贺知章, 659 – 744), a famous poet of the Tang Dynasty, a friend of Li Bai's

3 mandarin: an official at traditional Chinese court, often used derogatively in this kind of context

4 brocade: embroidery

5 aftermath: consequence (usually bad, or undesirable)

6 sheaves of song: a great number of bundles of poems ("sheaf" singular form)

7 a jugful: a jug full (of wine in this context)

8 Sovereign: highest power, or ruler of a state

9 Imperial barge: the boat or ship for the king

10 Keats: John Keats (1795 – 1821) English romantic poet

11 Liu Ling: (刘伶, 221 – 300), a Chinese poet and scholar. One of the seven sages of the bamboo grove, Liu Ling was a Daoist who retreated to the countryside in order to pursue a spontaneous and natural existence that would be impossible under the tight controls of the imperial court. Popularly regarded as eccentric, he was notorious for his love of alcohol.

12 imprisonment, condemnation to death, pardon: In fact, Li Bai was imprisoned briefly due to An Lushan Rebellion, condemned to exile, and later pardoned in Hubei province when he was in the middle of the journey. Upon hearing the news of the imperial pardon, he immediately returned, composing one of his most famous poems in celebration of his new life *Through the Three Gorges of the Yangtze River* (《早发白帝城》).

13 mulan: the name of a precious wood

14 merman: a mythical male legendary creature who has a human form from the waist up, and is fishlike from the waist down. It is less commonly known than its female counterpart, mermaid.

15 Chu'ping: Qu Yuan (屈原，332 – 295), a loyal minister under Huai Wang, the ruler of the Chu State. He was famous for his poem *Li Sao* (《离骚》).

16 Chu Kings: rulers of the state Chu

1 ▷ Comprehension work

1. What problem made emperor so angry at his ministers one day?
2. How did Li Bai help the emperor solve his problem?
3. How did the emperor reward Li Bai, and how did the poet treat this reward?
4. What are the ways of love in which Li Bai became practiced when he turned twenty?
5. What was his life like in terms of his marriage, financial conditions, and personal relationship?
6. Why did Li Bai reply "Please your Majesty, I'm a god of wine"? What does this reply mean?
7. Why was the legend unsatisfied at a normal death of a great poet, and wanted to create a more poetic death for Li Bai? Do you think Li Bai would be happy about this story?

2 ▷ A literary study

Work in small groups to answer the following question:

How is Li Bai's romantic image created through describing his life about LOVE, MARRIAGE, MONEY, AUTHORITY, EQUALITY, POETRY, and DEATH?

Read the article carefully to select evidence to support your judgements.

In-depth reading	
No.	**Li Bai's romantic image**
1	LOVE:
2	MARRIAGE:
3	MONEY:
4	AUTHORITY:
5	EQUALITY:
6	LOVE for WINE:
7	POETRY:
8	DEATH:

Mini-critique writing

What does the last poem say about the character of the poet? Read it carefully and write a short essay in about 200 words.

My ship is built of spice-wood and has a rudder of mulan;
Musicians sit at the two ends with jeweled bamboo flutes and pipes of gold.
What a pleasure it is, with a cask of sweet wine and singing girls beside me,
To drift on the water hither and thither with the waves!
I am happier than the fairy of the air, who rode on his yellow crane,
And free as the merman who followed the sea-gulls aimlessly.
Now with the strokes of my inspired pen I shake the Five Mountains.
My poem is done, I laugh, and my delight is vaster than the sea.
Oh, deathless poetry! The songs of Chu'ping are ever glorious as the sun and moon.
While the palaces and towers of the Chu kings have vanished from hills.

 Language work

Paraphrase the following sentences.

1. "What!" exclaimed the emperor, "among so many magistrates, so many scholars and warriors, cannot there be found a single one who knows enough to relieve us of vexation in this affair? If in three days no one is able to decipher this letter, every one of your appointments shall be suspended."

    _____

    _____

2. ... then Minister He Zhizhang approached the throne and said: "Your subject presumes to announce to your Majesty that there is a poet of great merit called Li at his house, who is perfectly acquainted with more than one science; command him to read this letter, for there is nothing of which he is not capable."

    _____

    _____

3. Having read the message, he dictated a learned and terrifying answer, which the emperor signed, almost believing He, that Li was an angel descended from heaven.

    _____

    _____

4. In the end, after imprisonment, condemnation to death, pardon, and every experiment in suffering, he found his way to his childhood home, only to die three years afterward. Legend, unsatisfied with a common end for so extraordinary a soul, told how he was drowned in a river while attempting to embrace the water's reflection of the moon.

    _____

    _____

5 > Vocabulary work

Study the words in the box below, and use them to complete the sentences. Make changes if you think it is necessary.

confer	chaos	fear	present
enamored	fret	relieve	height

1. He was at the _____ of fame when he died.
2. The government finally had to reform its financial system in the _____ of economic crisis.
3. She signed the contract that would _____ him of all the debt in his company.
4. The mother _____ for her son's safety when he set out to the desert for explorations.
5. The children returned safely with the help of the teachers. It turned out that nothing is to _____ about.
6. The policy requires every applicant to _____ themselves to the officer in the office when they apply for a visa.
7. The tourists were completely _____ of the beauty of the scene, and the people of the little island.
8. The celebrity is said to have got his PhD degree from a diploma mill which means a university that _____ the degree upon anybody who pays the expensive tuition fees.

PART 3 Extended Activities

1 > Dictation

2 > Read more

Sophia Loren and Me
By Pieter-Dirk Uys

Who says dreams can't come true? When I was a kid growing up in South Africa, my hero was Prime Minister Hendrik Verwoerd, and his picture was on my wall. Then I bought a copy of *Stage and Cinema* and discovered a beautiful Italian girl called Sophia Loren. Her legs were better than those of our prime minister, so she took his place. She's been there ever since.

I went to Rome for the first time at age 16, and, armed with a magazine picture in my hand, went searching for Sophia. In the picture she was leaning out of a window, waving at the camera with, as background, an ornate lamppost and a Roman ruin. So I looked all over Rome and found the lamppost.

She wasn't home. I left a note: "dear Miss Loren, I'm from Cape Town, and I love you."

When I got home, there was a letter from her, personal, sweet, and with an address, so I wrote back. We started an extraordinary pen friendship, with me at first gushing my admiration and she sweetly thanking. But as I grew up and other things happened, I would write about them.

When my mother died suddenly, I had to take command of my devastated family and could find no time to mourn. I wrote to Sophia, and her letter to me gave the comfort I needed so badly.

I went to live in London in the late 1960s, and wrote her a movie script while at the London Film School. She responded with a very detailed discussion of it, telling me why she didn't think it was right for her, but encouraging me to keep working. "Nothing is easy," she wrote.

I came back to South Africa and started writing, always keeping her in mind for every character I created. And yet it was all so wrong for her. She couldn't play Afrikaans matriarchs, Afrikaans daughters or Afrikaans mothers.

In 1974 I was in Paris, and dropped her a present of South African tea at her apartment, leaving the name of the hotel where I was staying. She phoned and invited me to visit her. When she walked into the room and I met her for the first

Notes

1. Pieter-Dirk Uys: a South African writer, actor and political satirist

2. Sophia Loren (1934 –): a leading Italian film actress; she has appeared in such films as *Two Women* (1961), *Yesterday, Today, and Tomorrow* (1963), and *A Very Special Day* (1977).

3. Hendrik Verwoerd (1901 – 1966): the late South African prime minister (1958 – 1966). He was assassinated in Cape Town.

4. Winnie Mandela (1934 –): South African political leader, former wife of Nelson Mandela, the first black president of South Africa.

5. Desmond Tutu (1931 –): South African religious leader. He advocates non-violence and interracial reconciliation. In 1984, he was awarded the Nobel Peace Prize.

6. Margaret Thatcher (1925 –): British Conservative politician who served as prime minister from 1979 to 1990.

7. John Major (1943 –): British Conservative politician, prime minister (1990 – 1997).

8. Afrikaans (*n*): a language that developed from the 17th-century Dutch and is one of the official languages of South Africa. It is a Germanic language of the Indo-European family. (*adj*): of or relating to Afrikaans or Afrikaners.

9. Afrikaner (*n*): an Afrikaans-speaking South African of European ancestry, especially one descended from 17th-century Dutch settlers.

time, it was as if a color picture from *Stage and Cinema* had peeled off my wall and come to life.

Her children came to look at the stamps I brought them. "An elephant's tooth!" Eduardo cooed, holding the stamp of the tall concrete Taalmonument upside down.

"No, that's the Afrikaans Language Monument," I said. We looked at it solemnly.

"A monument for the Afrikaans language?" asked Sophia Loren. I nodded proudly. "Why? Is it dead?"

Since then we've seen each other whenever we've been in the same city, but, until recently, she'd never seen my live show. She and her family always enjoyed the videos in which I satirized political figures such as Winnie Mandela, Bishop Desmond Tutu, Maggie Thatcher and John Major. So when I had my performance in Los Angeles in April 1993, I rang her at her ranch and said, "I'm here. Can you come?" And there I was, doing my satire called "Stand Up South Africa!" to a packed 800-strong audience. In the third row sat the face from my wall.

She came backstage at the interval, and her beauty, warmth and familiarity were astounding. After the show she brought her son Eduardo backstage, the baby now a man.

It was a wonderful moment when it was all over and everyone had left the dressing room. My Winnie, Desmond, Maggie, and Major costumes were back in their boxes, and I could stand outside the theater and look at the famous Hollywood sign on the hill. I saw a 13-year-old blond Afrikaans boy take down a photograph of a prime minister from his wall and replace it with that of a smiling Italian film star. And 35 years later her perfume was still around me, the touch of her lips still on my face.

Who said Hollywood dreams can't come true?

A True / False / Not Mentioned (NM).

1. The writer first met Sophia Loren when he was 16.
2. When they became pen friends, he expressed his admiration for Sophia in his letters.
3. Sophia wrote letters to him because she liked the South African kid.
4. Sophia tried to act some Afrikaans characters in the films.
5. In Paris, he was invited to Sophia's home to perform some shows.
6. Sophia watched his performance in Los Angeles in April, 1993.
7. The friendship between him and Sophia lasted for 35 years.

B Topics for discussion.

1. What was the dream of the narrator?
2. Did the narrator's dream come true? Give your reasons.
3. Do you have any dreams? What is it?

Grammar work

Correct the mistakes in the following sentences.

1. Sade will not be bothered too much, she can enjoy her private life in the small village.
2. Provide Sade follows the new fashion, millions of fickle British pop fans will love her again.
3. If any visitors could come, I'll say you aren't here.
4. In case a fire, ring the alarm bell immediately.
5. When will you be back at the office? — I'll be back until 10 o'clock.
6. Tomorrow it is going to rain. You will be sorry unless you don't take an umbrella.
7. Let me know when will you arrive.
8. Will there be a picnic tomorrow? — Yes, there will if it doesn't rain.
9. I will come if only nothing is said to the teacher.

 Word formation

Fill in the following blanks with derivatives of the words in brackets.

1. Although they are rivals in the competition, they never showed open _____ (hostile) to each other.
2. They decided to help the _____ (able) child who lost one of her legs in a traffic accident.
3. Owing to the _____ (obscure) of the language, few people are able to understand this novel.
4. Since he treated my complaint with _____ (indifferent), I had to take the case to court at last.
5. In order to promote the new product, they launched _____ (public) campaigns in several business districts.
6. The _____ (resemble) between the two boys is so great that no one can tell one from the other.
7. His _____ (familiar) with the local languages surprised me.

> *dis* — a prefix added to adjectives, adverbs, nouns and verbs, meaning negative, reverse or opposite of, e.g. dishonest , disagreeably, disagreement, disengage.
>
> *-ity* — a suffix added to adjectives to form nouns, e.g. purity, oddity.
>
> *-ance, -ence* — suffixes added to verbs to form nouns, meaning the action or state of the stated verb, e.g. assistance, confidence.

 Vocabulary work

Praise or criticism?

Match the following idiomatic expressions in bold type with the interpretations in the right column.

1. When it comes to modern jazz music, she's really **on the ball**.	a. very good

2. That female actress thought she was **God's gift**, and the attitude really offended the press.

3. Bill **has a way with** those naughty children. Other teachers envy him.

4. Sade hasn't released a single song for four years. But she complains about the drop of her popularity. She **wants jam on it**!

5. You shouldn't **run down** your country when you are abroad.

6. I am fascinated by Michael's songs but I don't like his performance. He was often dressed up like **a dog's dinner**.

7. She is a really **first rate** teacher, the very best in our school.

8. Marie has really got **green fingers**; look at those flowers!

b. have totally unreasonable expectations and demands

c. over-dressed in a showy way

d. good at establishing relations and motivating them

e. very attractive to the opposite sex

f. knowing a lot, well informed

g. good at gardening

h. criticize

6 Writing

Write an essay on *Poetry in My University* in about 300 words based on the results of the survey with the questions below.

Questions for the survey

⭐ Who are reading poetry in your university?

⭐ Who is their favorite poet?

⭐ What are their favorite poems?

⭐ Do they think poetry is getting out of fashion with young people today? Why?

Cultural Information

Read the passage below, and then complete the task of cultural study.

Landmark Pop Stars

"Pop" is short for "popular" and there has always been popular music. But until the 1950s there wasn't a style of music just for young people. That all changed when rock and roll began. Since then, hundreds of styles and stars have come and gone. Here, we look at the highlights of a few rock and pop landmark stars.

1. The Rolling Stones: This is a British rock music group which was formed in the 1960s and later made successful tours in the US. The group still sometimes plays together, and the best known member is Mick Jagger. The Stones were unsmiling singers, singing rough rock. They were usually dressed like hippies.

2. The Beatles: Very successful British pop group of four musicians, John Lennon, Paul McCartney, George Harrison and Ringo Strarr. The group was formed in the early 1960s. Unlike the Rolling Stones, their songs are sweet and melodic. They include *"Yesterday"*, *"Yellow Submarine"*, *"I Want to Hold Your Hand and Help"*, written mostly by John Lennon and McCartney. When the Beatles separated in 1970, each member of the group continued to work in pop music. In 1980, John Lennon was murdered in the US. In 1996, there was a new interest across the Western world in the music of the Beatles. New CDs, videos and films were released, and the remaining members of the group were interviewed on TV.

3. Elvis Presley (1935 – 1977) (猫王): Elvis Presley was an American singer and guitar player who made rock and roll popular in the 1950s. On his death in 1977, US president Carter said, "Elvis Presley changed the face of American popular culture ... he was unique and irreplaceable." He recorded his first songs in Memphis at the age of 19. Now many people connect Memphis with pop music and especially with Elvis Presley. From 1956 – 1963, he was the most successful and influential person in popular music. And he was even nicknamed King of Rock. He was sometimes called "Elvis the Pelvis" because of the way he moved the lower half of his body during his performances. His many successful records include *"Heartbreak Hotel"* and *"Don't Be Cruel"*, and he also appeared in films, including *"Loving You"* and *"G I Blues"*.

4. Michael Jackson (1958 – 2009): An Afro-American popular music singer and songwriter, the youngest brother of the group The Jackson Five who had many hit records in the 1970s. Michael Jackson on his own won great success in the 1980s, with the albums *"Thriller and Bad"*, and his performances in concerts. People often talk about the fact that he has had his face greatly changed by plastic surgery.

Cultural Study Task

Ask 20 students among your classmates on their knowledge of cultural celebrities in China and the rest of the world. Use the questions below for the survey.

How many students can name:

(1) Three western pop stars? _____

(2) Three Chinese pop stars? _____

(3) Three western movie stars? _____

(4) Three Chinese movie stars? _____

(5) Three western poets? _____

(6) Three Chinese poets? _____

(7) Three western novelists? _____

(8) Three Chinese novelists? _____

(9) One western pop song title? _____

(10) One Chinese pop song title ? _____

(11) One western movie title? _____

(12) One Chinese movie title? _____

(13) One favorite English poem? _____

(14) One favorite Chinese poem? _____

(15) One modern novel by a western author? _____

(16) One modern novel by a Chinese author? _____

Now, analyze your results, and discuss what they tell us about the cultural life of modern Chinese university students.

Teenager's Nightmare

Introduction

In this unit, you will learn to use English for

▶ Giving direct command
▶ Talking about both positive and negative aspects of school education
▶ Writing about school examination systems in China, UK, and US

PART 1 Communicative Activities

1 ▷ Interactive listening and speaking

A Listening

In this part, you will hear a talk between father and son about study. What would they

say? Now, listen and then complete the following tasks.

Select the correct answer to each of the following questions.

1. What did the father command his son to do?
    a. To tell him what his son's favorite subject is in the new school.
    b. To tell him the results of examinations.
    c. To tell him what sports the son takes recently.
2. What did the father think of the scores?
    a. He wasn't impressed.
    b. He was disappointed.
    c. He was overjoyed.
3. Why didn't the son do well in the exam?
    a. He had his own idea of life.
    b. He hated school life.
    c. He didn't have good teachers.
4. What rules did the father lay down for his son?
    a. Limiting TV watching to no more than an hour.
    b. Going to bed by ten o'clock.
    c. Study at least an hour every night.

B **Reading and debating.**

It is believed by many that a strict parent would turn out a promising child. For example, one mother found that her daughter came in the second place in a math examination in her class. She then forced her daughter to practice 2000 problems before allowing her to go to bed. This philosophy is also believed by some teachers. For instance, one teacher required his pupil who made a mistake in spelling to copy the word 100 times.

But numerous people argue that such a style of teaching only reflects the parent or teacher badly. They try to avoid teaching the most important things in life, which are more challenging, and more difficult to develop, but more important for the future of children. Read the following excerpt from an American writer, and then take a side to debate. Which is more difficult and more important to learn? Knowledge from the book or social skills gained through social activities?

It is argued that practicing copying or doing 2000 math problems "requires focused attention," but it is "nowhere near as cognitively demanding as" social activities. "Managing status rivalries, negotiating group dynamics, understanding social norms, navigating the distinction between self and group — these and other social tests impose cognitive demands that blow away any intense tutoring session or a class at Yale."

One writer argues that mastering these arduous skills is at the very essence of achievement. Most people work in groups. We do this because groups are much more efficient at solving problems than individuals. Moreover, the performance of a group does not correlate well with the average IQ of the group of even the IQ's of the smartest members.

Researchers at the Massachusetts Instutite of Technology and Carnegie Mellon have found that groups have a high collective intelligence when members of a group are good at reading each others' motions — when they take turns speaking, when the inputs from each member are managed fluidly, when they detect each others' inflinations and strengths.

Participating in a well-functioning group is really hard. It requires the ability to trust people outside your kinship circle, read intonations and moods, understand how the psychological pieces each person brings to the room can and cannot fit together.

This skill set is not taught formally, but it is imparted through arduous experiences. These are exactly the kinds of difficult experinces that those teachers and parents shelter their children and students from by making them rush home to hit the homework table.

(Based on David Brooks *Amy Chua Is a Whimp**)

With this background infomration, take a side in one of the following boxes, to prepare for a debate.

Knowledge or social skills: Which one is more important for our future?		
For Knowledge		For Social Skills

* Published on Jan 17, 2011, *The New York Times*.

2 > What are they for?

There are many ways to express commands. Read the following sentences and match the functions with the actual words spoken.

Actual words spoken	Functions
a. Do you mind not making so much noise? b. Follow me. c. You must be careful. d. You mustn't smoke in the office. e. You're to stay here until I return. f. Jack and Susan stand over there! g. Faster! h. Not so fast! i. Do you object to cleaning the room for the party?	1. You tell Jack and Susan to stand over there. 2. You ask someone to follow you. 3. You ask someone not to move so fast. 4. You ask someone to keep quiet. 5. You tell someone not to smoke in the office. 6. You ask someone to be careful. 7. You ask someone to move faster. 8. You tell someone to stay there until you come back. 9. You try to get somebody to clean the room.

3 > More sentences

1. This way!

2. Bring it here.

3. Mike, Billy and Tom, you form a group and discuss this topic.

4. Will you be quiet!

5. Do eat up your din-din.

6. Go ahead!

7. Somebody let me out.

8. Off you go!

9. Down your leg!

10. Up you come!

Matching Exercise

a. Ask your children to finish their dinner. _____

b. Ask Mike, Billy and Tom to form a group and discuss this topic. _____

c. Ask your child to go. _____

157

d. Ask your friend to come up. _____

e. Encourage someone to go forward. _____

f. Request someone to be quiet. _____

g. Request people to let you out. _____

h. Ask someone to go in the direction pointed out. _____

i. Ask your child to put down his or her leg. _____

j. Ask someone to bring it here. _____

Proverb

No Pains, no gains.

PART 2 Reading and Language Activities

Text Football

▶ Pre-reading tasks **Discuss the following questions.**

1. Do you like school examinations, why or why not?

2. What are the stages of going through an examination?

3. How do you feel when you take an examination? Tick your answers from the following list:

apprehensive	panic	nervous	worried	frightened
excited	amazed	terrible	joyous	scared

▶ Read the text

Taking exams must be one of the most frightening experiences that anyone must go through. It is not so much the actual taking of the exams themselves which is so awful, although of course they play a great part in the general feeling of fear; no, the most awful time comes at the beginning and at the end.

The beginning is the time when you are meant to revise. Revision is a terrible time both if you revise and if you don't. Firstly, if you revise, concentrating on a pile of A4 pages covered in your untidy handwriting, you suddenly wish not only that you had written everything down a bit more clearly, but also that you had started revision a lot earlier. However, once resigned to the fact that you can't put the clock back, you prepare to give yourself up to full and thorough revision, putting aside all else in life. Of course, such a hard decision is absolutely impossible to carry out, although you do try to fool yourself that you can undertake it easily. You let your attention wander away easily, finding you have a sudden, irresistible urge to tidy up your room, even though it has looked like a pigsty for the last three months.

When you are tempted away from your studying by such strange amusements, you are moving onto the territory of the second group concerning revision — those who know they need and should get down to hard studying, but somehow have neither got the determination nor the willpower to force themselves to sit down for hours on end digesting the delights of pure mathematics. Now, this second group in which we have all found ourselves from time to time suffer the most severe guilt complexes over their lack of revision. Although they are aware that they should be studying they cannot somehow bring themselves to the awful task; temptation has won over what they know they should be doing , and in a way they suffer far more than those who eventually find the willpower and determination to sit down and revise.

The end of the exam procedure, which is in some cases worse than the revision period, is awaiting the results. While waiting you can't do much about your own school work. You feel that it is very hard to resist the temptation to light a fire with all your notebooks and files instead of logs, but at the same time you feel that you had better keep all your notes safe in case you discover you have failed and need to re-take all your subjects. The worst day of all is the one when you know that the postman is to deliver the letter (always in a brown envelope to make it look more official and frightening) which will inform you whether the academic world (and society in general)considers you a failure or a success, whether you can get the job you want, or go to the university you wish to attend. That envelope is to contain the key to your future and, perhaps most importantly of all, to inform you whether you need to suffer again the horrors of exams.

1 ▷ Comprehension work

A Read the text again and discuss the following questions.

1. What are the troubles for those who revise before an exam?
2. What is meant by the sentence "you can't put the clock back"?
3. What does the expression "strange amusements" refer to?
4. What is the main problem faced by the second group — those who don't revise?
5. Why does the writer have a desire "to light a fire with all your notebooks and files"? Why can't he do that?
6. Why does the letter in a brown envelope seem so important to an examinee?

B Activity

Some people argue that school examinations are "nightmares for students". And they have launched a campaign to "do away with them." You take the supporting side and your partner takes the opposing side.

You may use the following cues to argue with each other. See if you can reach an agreement.

Supporting side	Opposing side
• exams — nightmares, terrible, painful experiences • dilemma at the beginning, revision or no revision • guilt complexes over lack of revision • suspense in waiting for the exam results	• exams — necessary for measuring what has been learnt • no pains, no gains — persistent effort to learn more • revision — another opportunity for learning • exam results — not the last judgement

2 ▶ Language work

A Fill in the following blanks with words or phrases from the text.

1. In revision, some boys have trouble _____ on their books and _____. They always find something nearby that distracts their attention. They are _____ to glance at the football match on the screen or the sensational stories in newspapers. The _____ is so strong that it seems almost _____ to most boys. They simply do not have the _____ to go on with their study. The best way is to keep them in a room free from any distraction. For a moment their attention may still _____ away from their work. But soon they would _____ themselves to the fact that they could do nothing except _____ _____ to business.

2. As one of the most important _____ in education, exams are aimed to evaluate how well students have learnt their _____, not to make them _____.

3. In Britain, educating children at home has become increasingly popular. Many parents think that school curriculum and exams that all pupils have to _____ _____ do not suit each individual child. They work out particular programs _____ the ordinary business of day-to-day life and responding to children's interests and questions. To _____ _____ these programs, parents make some adjustments which enable their kids to _____ the courses more easily. This practice is called "Education Otherwise".

4. In US, high school graduates first apply for admission to the university they wish to _____. The university's decision is based on the applicants' _____ performance in high school and their scores of SAT (Scholastic Aptitude Test).

B Rewrite the following sentences with the words and expressions in the box.

get down to	territory	undertake	temptation
in case	give oneself up to	resign oneself to	on end
an urge to do something	carry out		

1. Elias Howe devoted his whole energy to the design of a sewing machine.

_____

2. The singer specializes in classic music. Pop music is outside his area of interest.

_____

3. Armed with modern equipment, the police took on the difficult job of looking for the missing boy in the woods.

_____

4. Due to lack of funds, the scientists found it difficult to put the plan into operation.

_____

5. Toys in bright colors usually have a strong attraction for children.

_____

6. You may use this police hot-line if it should happen that someone tries to break in.

_____

7. Tired of intense publicity, the movie star has a strong desire to live on a desert island.

_____

8. Sade's debut album was so successful that it stayed in the Top Ten Charts continuously for months.

_____

9. We've spent so much time talking, now let's begin to work hard on the project.

_____

10. The woman accepted the fact that she would never get the call from the man.

_____

C Word study.

   a. **Give the meanings of the following words or expressions used in the text. You may use an English-English Dictionary. Then give a sentence to illustrate their meanings and usage.**

   1. go through

   _____

   2. be meant to

   _____

   3. have an urge to

   _____

   4. in case

   _____

5. concentrate on

_____

6. resign oneself to

_____

b. Each of the following clues has an example sentence. Use the prompts to produce other sentences with the same pattern as the example.

1. Prompt: exam / frightening experience / go through

   Example: Taking exams must be one of the most frightening experiences that anyone must go through.

   a. he / not / want / marry / again / because not / want / go through

   b. said / person / mature / without / go through / hardships

   c. boy / go through / notes / before / exam

2. Prompt: beginning / time / be meant to / revise

   Example: The beginning is the time when you are meant to revise.

   a. teachers / be meant to / treat / pupils like parents

   b. soldiers / be meant to / defend

   c. in Japan / people / be meant to / take off shoes / before entering their homes

3. Prompt : you / find / have an urge / to

   Example: You find you have a sudden, irresistible urge to tidy up your room.

   a. he / have a sudden urge / ride the horse

   b. the old man / alone / have an urge to / talk to someone

   c. girl / waiting / have an irresistible urge / call her boyfriend

4. Prompt: you / feel / you / keep / notes / in case / discover / failed / and retake / subjects

   Example: You feel that you had better keep all your notes safe in case you discover you have failed and need to retake all your subjects.

   a. you / take / umbrella / in case

   b. before the joint project / begin / everything / write down / in case / dispute

   c. you / put away / laptop / in case / children / touch

5. Prompt: concentrate on / A4 pages / the student / wish that

   Example: Concentrating on a pile of A4 pages covered in his / her untidy handwriting, the student suddenly wished that he had written everything down a bit more clearly.

   a. concentrate on the microscope / the scientist / make a sudden discovery / new organism

   b. concentrate on / novel / he / barely / notice / getting dark

   c. when / hungry / can't / concentrate on / work

6. Prompt: resigned to / fact / you / not put / clock / back / you / prepare to

   Example: Resigned to the fact that you can't put the clock back, you prepare to give yourself up to full and thorough revision.

   a. resigned to / unable / walk / she / learn to use wheelchair

b. I / have to / resign myself to / fact / have lost the job / so / find a new one

c. he / look / calmly / resigned to / fate

PART 3 Extended Activities

1 Dictation

2 Read more

Kids Will Be Kids — If We Let Them By Arthur Black

One of the most obvious facts about grown-ups to a child is that they have forgotten about what it is like to be a child.

— Randall Jarrell

Ana Cross of Nanaimo, BC, would know all about that. Recently Ana was busted by a city bylaw enforcement officer for illegally operating a business on city property. The officer wrote her up and closed her down.

The business was a lemonade stand that Ana has been running by the road outside her house since she was seven. Ana is ten years old.

It isn't the bylaw control office that's at fault — they get a complaint, they have to act on it. What ticks me off is that Ana Cross has a neighbor so narrow-minded and flint-hearted that he or she derived satisfaction from siccing the law on a child.

For what — being too grown-up for her age?

Could be. Maturity and responsibility are not character traits we encourage in our young ones these days. According to an article in *USA Today*, many American schools have found a brand-new bogeyman — red ink.

School administrators have determined that the trauma of seeing a large, red X through

163

a wrong answer on a test paper or examination might prove to be too "stressful, demeaning, even frightening" for the tender psyches of school-aged children. Teachers are being urged to go back to their Crayola boxes and opt for "more pleasant" colors such as green, orange or purple.

Concern for school kids' fragile sensibilities extends to the playground. The games of tag and dodge ball have been banned from several American schoolyards on the grounds that they are "too competitive." The principal of a Santa Monica, California, elementary school finds the game of tag particular repugnant. "In this game," she says, "there is a 'victim' who is designated as 'It'. This creates a self-esteem issue."

Some educators say that all competitive sports, from soccer and baseball to marbles and musical chairs, should be tossed out in favor of "affirmative" sports like, well, pogo sticking, juggling and — er, that's about it, really.

If the folks at the Tufts Educational Day Care Center in Massachusetts have their way, kids will be preconditioned long before they even get to grade one. At Tufts, preschoolers are required to agree to a contract that reads in part: "I —, know how to listen to my teachers. When my teachers talk to me, I will not scream, try to hit, or say 'You're not my boss.' If I do any of these things, I will go to the sensory loft so I can slow down my heart." Presumably each child will be appointed a lawyer with power of attorney since they won't yet have learned to read or write.

Don't feel smug, Canucks — things are just goofy this side of the border. Not long ago, the North York Women Teachers' Association in Ontario published a brochure calling for the removal of "violent" and "militaristic" language in classroom. The brochure replaces expressions such as "killing two

Notes

1. About the author: Arthur Black is a Canadian writer. The article is adapted from his book *Grindstone*, published by Harbor Publishing Co. Ltd, 2007.

2. Nanaimo, BC: a small city in the Province of British Columbia (BC), Canada

3. *USA Today*: a US national newspaper

4. Crayola: a brand of crayons

5. tag and dodge ball: two forms of games which involve rough physical contacts between players

6. togo sticking: a game played with a device called pogo stick for jumping off the ground in a standing position with the aid of a spring, used as a toy or exercise equipment

7. sensory loft: a corner in a room or an attic in the top of a house (where the children can be asked to stay away from other activities as a form of punishment for disobedience)

8. Jonah and the whale: It is a biblical story in which Jonah, asked by God to preach among the enemies, ran away from the task. Because of this he fell into a disaster of being swallowed up by a whale. In spite of his defiance, God saved him by ordering the whale to spit him out onto the shore. When saved, Jonah became an obedient servant of God. The story preaches a lesson of obedience, and repentance.

9. Canucks: my Canadian folks (humorous)

birds with one stone" and "take a stab at it" with Milquetoast bromides like "getting two for the price of one" and "go for it."

Even the lowly computer did not escape North York Newspeak. The brochure urged teachers to instruct their students always to "press", not "hit" the computer keys.

If, like me, you think the brave new world of educational hyper-sensitivity is a little bit much, be of good cheer. We're not alone. Mrs. Sarah Goldberg of New York City is in our corner.

Each school day Mrs. Goldberg sent her son to a rather exclusive elementary school on Manhattan's West Side. And every day she sent with Jonah a cartoon of a smiling, spouting whale that she drew on the brown paper bag that contained his lunch. (The son's name was Jonah. Jonah and the whale — geddit?) Each morning, Jonah would put his lunch bag with all the other kids' lunch bags, and each day at noon, the teacher would distribute all the lunches. Because of the whale, Jonah and his friends knew which lunch was Jonah's and they thought it was very cool.

The teacher disagreed. Mrs. Goldberg got a telephone call from her son's teacher asking her to stop drawing the whale on the lunch bag because it was "unfair" to children with less pictogram-friendly names.

The next day, Jonah arrived at school with the usual whale-festooned lunch bag and a note to the teacher. The note reads: "The Goldberg family whale policy will continue. Tell the other kids to get over it."

A Answer these questions.

a. What are the author's attitudes to these people and things or rules?
  a) Sympathetic
  b) Supportive
  c) Scathing
  d) Sarcastic
  e) Indifferent
  f) Humorous

People, things, or rules	His attitudes
1. 10 years old Ana Cross whose lemonade was closed down	
2. The city bylaw enforcement officer who wrote Ana up, and closed her stand down	
3. Ana's neighbor who lodged a complaint to the city bylaw office	
4. The call for the teachers to use more colorful crayons instead of a red X on wrong answers	
5. The banning of competitive games such as tag or dodge ball	
6. Games such as juggling and togo sticking	

7. The alleged contract for preschool children at Tufts, US	
8. The call for removing violent or militaristic language such as "killing two birds with one stone" or "take a stab at it"	
9. The call for using "press" instead of "hit" in using the computer	
10. The lunch bag with Jonah and the whale drawing	
11. The teacher's request to stop drawing Jonah and the whale on the lunch bag	
12. Mrs. Goldberg's note: "The Goldberg family whale policy will continue. Tell the other kids to get over it."	

b. What is his major argument of this essay?

a) Some schools know how to treat children like children, but some don't.

b) Grownups often forget children are children. All the cases cited in the article support this point of view.

c) Schools in US know better than those in Canada about how to treat children like children.

d) Schools in Canada know better than those in US about how to treat children like children.

 3 Grammar work

Correct the mistakes in the following sentences.

1. You ought to not see him any more.

2. You're not supposed playing the ball games in the classroom.

3. "It's raining. You would take the umbrella with you," said the mother.

4. The guest requested: "I could like to have another drink."

5. The doctor said seriously to the patient: "You've got a bad cough, so you can't smoke a cigarette any more."

6. At the meeting, the chairman suggested that the present examination system will be reformed.

7. "John, where is your sister? You would have brought her to the party. She is welcome here."

8. "Professor Davy, may you write a recommendation letter for me"?

9. If you see a man with a black cap appear before that building, you can call the police immediately, OK?

 4 Word formation

Fill in the following blanks with derivatives of the words in brackets.

1. Two ships came into _____ (collide) near the seaport this morning.

2. The committee had a heated _____ (discuss) before they arrived at a _____ (decide).

3. The students are doing some final _____ (revise) for the entrance exam.

4. The sweets on the table were too strong a _____ (tempt) for the child to resist.

5. They asked her to help them in physics and she agreed without the slightest _____ (hesitate).

6. Her _____ (determine) to learn English was not weakened by the difficulties she met with.

> *-ion* is a suffix added to verbs to form nouns showing action or condition of the stated verb, e.g. confession. Some variations of *-ion* are *-ation*, *-ition*, *-sion*, *-tion*, e.g., hesitate — hesitation, compete — competition, admit — admission, dictate — dictation.

5 ▶ Vocabulary work

Fill in the following blanks with the given words in an appropriate form.

1. The present situation is _____ (terrify) and everybody in the town is _____ (terrify).

2. The _____ (satisfy) customer thanked me.

3. There is nothing very _____ (surprise) in this.

4. She was quite _____ (astonish) at his behavior.

5. The scientists are _____ (please) with the results.

6. He became even more _____ (depress) after his wife died.

7. I had nothing to do. I was _____ (bore) and lonely.

8. Mary looked calm, but inside she felt really _____ (excite).

9. Was it an _____ (excite) game?
   Yes, very _____ (thrill).

10. Was it _____ (interest)?
    Yes , it was _____ (fascinate).

11. When you find something funny, you are _____ (amuse) by it.

12. We were dreadfully late. It was very _____ (embarrass).

6 ▶ Cloze

Fill in each blank with an appropriate word.

> ### Perfect Answers
>
> The following concerns a question in a physics degree exam at the University of Copenhagen.
>
> "Describe how to determine the height of a skyscraper with a barometer."
>
> One student replied:
>
> "You tie a long piece of string to the neck of the barometer, then lower the barometer from the roof of the (1) _____ to the ground. The length of the string plus the length

of the barometer will equal the height of the building."

This highly original answer so incensed the examiner that the student was failed. The student appealed on the (2) _____ that his answer was indisputably correct, and the university appointed an independent arbiter to decide the case. The (3) _____ judged that the answer was indeed correct, but didn't do the problem directly. So it was decided to call the student in and allow him six minutes (4) _____ which to provide a verbal answer which showed at least a minimal familiarity with the basic principles of physics.

For five minutes the student sat in silence, forehead creased in thought. The arbiter reminded him that (5) _____ was running out, to which the student replied that he had several extremely relevant answers, but (6) _____ make up his mind which to use.

On being advised to hurry up the student replied as follows:

"Firstly, you could take the barometer up to the roof of the skyscraper, (7) _____ it over the edge, and measure the time it takes to reach the ground. The height of the building can then be worked out from the (8) _____ H = 0.5g x t squared. But bad luck on the barometer."

"Or if the sun is shining you could (9) _____ the height of the barometer, then set it on end and measure the length of its shadow. Then you measure the length of the skyscraper's (10) _____, and thereafter it is a simple matter of proportional arithmetic to work out the height of the skyscraper."

"But if you wanted to be highly scientific about it, you could (11) _____ a short piece of string to the barometer and swing it like a (12) _____, first at ground level and then on the roof of the skyscraper. The height is worked out by the difference in the gravitational restoring force T = 2 pi sq root (l / g)."

"Or if the skyscraper has an outside emergency staircase, it would be easier to (13) _____ up it and mark off the height of the skyscraper in barometer lengths, then add them up."

"If you merely wanted to be boring and orthodox about it, of course, you could use the barometer to measure the air pressure on the roof of the skyscraper and on the ground, and convert the difference in millibars into feet to give the (14) _____ of the building."

"But since we are constantly being exhorted to exercise independence of mind and apply (15) _____ methods, undoubtedly the best way would be to knock on the janitor's door and say to him 'If you would like a nice new barometer, I will give you this one if you (16) _____ me the height of this skyscraper'."

The student was Niels Bohr, the only person from Denmark to win the Nobel prize for (17) _____.

7 ▶ Writing

A Work on your own.

There has been a lot of talk about the reform of national matriculation (录取) for tertiary education (高等教育). Why should we reform them and how? Write down your opinions and reasons. There are some hints in the brackets for your reference. You need not use them if you don't think they are appropriate.

E.g. (academic achievements / overall abilities)

The present system of examinations should be reformed because it emphasises only academic achievements rather than overall abilities.

1. (not fair to students specially gifted but not good in certain subjects)

   _____

2. (miss the fundamental aim of education, what is education for? for betterment of the person, for developing a person into a good citizen in society)

   _____

3. (encourage knowledge learning, neglect moral education)

   _____

4. (some students, having special needs, not reflected in the assessment)

   _____

5. (killing the creative spirit, producing millions of students who are patterned in thinking)

   _____

6. (waste of time in preparation for the test, forget everything afterwards)

   _____

B Write a short passage about your school.

 ## C ultural Information

Read the passage below, and then complete the task of cultural study.

Examinations in UK and US

In UK, there are two important types of qualification examinations for the students to take — GCSE (General Certificate of Secondary Education) and A-Level (Advanced Level) examinations. These examinations are not marked by school teachers, but by a special agency called "Examining Board." At the age of 15 or 16, students can take the GCSE examination, which shows whether they have successfully reached the level of secondary education. At 18, some students take the other type of examination — A-Level, usually in no more than three subjects. And the A-levels are necessary for anyone who wants to go to college or university.

In US, students also take examinations, both inside and outside school. But the inside examinations are not very important. Students do have examinations in the last two years of high school study. But the examination results are considered along with the other work that the students have done during the school years. For the students who hope to go to a university, they must take the SATs (the Scholastic Aptitude Tests), which are set as national examinations. A student's SAT results are presented to universities or colleges when students apply for entry, along with a record of the student's achievements at high school.

 Cultural Study Task

Write a paragraph in about 200 words describing the Chinese examination system, and how it is different from the American and British systems.

Have You Seen the Tree?

Introduction

In this unit, you will learn to use English for

▶ *Talking about one's beliefs, disbeliefs, and impressions*
▶ *Describing views*
▶ *Interpreting descriptions*

PART 1 Communicative Activities

1 ▶ Interactive listening and speaking

A Listening

In this conversation, you will hear two students talking on a topic "My Favorite

Season". Listen, and complete the following tasks.

1. What is Xiao Chen's favorite season?

   a. Spring

   b. Autumn

   c. Winter

2. Which aspects of this season seem to be particularly attractive?

   a. Everything comes back to life, which makes people more cheerful.

   b. There's a particular type of beauty on the ground in this season.

   c. The view is spectacular because of the multitude of trees planted in the city.

3. The view, though beautiful, is ephemeral because _____.

   a. seasons change rapidly

   b. human taste for beauty is precarious

   c. one has to experience it in person during a certain time of the day

4. It can be inferred from the conversation that the following statements are correct EXCEPT for _____.

   a. one student is now convinced that beauty can be found in the very commonplace things in our life

   b. one student usually gets up early while the other late in the morning

   c. one season is more beautiful than another

B Interactive speaking.

Beauty can be found in many commonplace things in almost every season. Now discuss the question in your group to complete the following table.

Seasons	Beauty that can be found in ...
Spring	
Summer	
Autumn	
Winter	

2 ▶ Poem and speaking

Read the poem, and then complete the tasks in groups.

Task 1

Complete the poem with the four lines below.
Sentences

    a) Of easy wind and downy flake
    b) To watch his woods fill up with snow
    c) But I have promise to keep
    d) Between the woods and frozen lake

Task 2

* Describe the scene where the poet speaker "sees", and what he "talks with his little horse".

* Interpret the last stanza "The woods are lovely ... before I sleep".

> **Note**
>
> Robert Frost: American poet (1874-1963). *Stopping by Woods on a Snowy Evening* is poet's one of the best loved poems.

Poem	Your answers to TASK 1 and 2
Stopping by Woods on a Snowy Evening *By Robert Frost* Whose woods these are I think I know. His house is in the village though; He will not see me stopping here (1) _____. My little horse must think it queer To stop without a farmhouse near (2) _____ The darkest evening of the year. He gives his harness bells a shake To ask if there is some mistake. The only other sound's the sweep (3) _____. The woods are lovely, dark and deep, (4) _____, And miles to go before I sleep, And miles to go before I sleep.	

3 ▷ What are they for?
Match the following functions to the actual words spoken.

Actual words spoken	Functions
a. I'll take your word for it. b. I'm convinced of Jack's honesty. c. I believe pen and paper will disappear by 2050. d. I'm going to resign — You must be joking. e. You've won the first prize in the competition! — Come on, don't pull my leg! f. I saw my cat talking to my neighbor's dog. —You can't be serious.	1. Say you would believe what someone has told you to be the best information available. 2. Say you believe that a revolutionary change will take place with our writing instruments. 3. Your friend says his cat talked to a dog. Say you don't believe his words. 4. Your friend tells you he will resign. Say you doubt his words. 5. Say you believe Jack is honest. 6. A friend tells you that you have won the first prize. Say you don't believe it.

 ## 4 ▷ More sentences
Read the following frequently used sentences and complete the matching exercise.

1. I'm determined to work harder during my last year at college. — I don't doubt your words.

2. Believe me, they left the room with the door unlocked. — I think what you said is true.

3. Tell you what, Jack worked real hard and passed the exam! — Seems believable.

4. Do you think I'd believe a story like that?

5. I found a huge frog in the garden. — Are you kidding?

6. I saw it, that big! — Don't tell me you've seen a rat in this house.

7. They've decided to move the petrol station out of town. — It can't be true.

9. Mark my words, guy. He won't deliver the goods to you if you pay him the money now. — Of course I won't. I wasn't born yesterday, was I?

8. They say the new motorway will bring bad luck to this town. — I don't believe a word of it.

Matching Exercise

a. Sentences of expressing belief: _____

b. Sentences of expressing disbelief: _____

Proverb

To sit in the shade on a fine day and look upon verdure is the most perfect refreshment.

PART 2 Reading and Language Activities

Text   Have You Seen the Tree?

▶ Pre-reading tasks **Discuss the following questions.**

1. Have you ever noticed a tree that truly touches you with its beautiful colors and shape?
2. Why do people sometimes fail to appreciate the beauty in ordinary things?
3. Have you ever been struck by any spectacular view in nature?

▶ Read the text

My neighbor Mrs. Gargan first told me about it. "Have you seen the tree?" she asked as I was sitting in the backyard enjoying the autumn twilight.

"The one down at the corner." She explained. "It's a beautiful tree — all kinds of colors. Cars are stopping to look. You ought to see it."

I told her I would, but I soon forgot about the tree. Three days later. I was jogging down the street, my mind swimming with petty worries, when a splash of bright orange caught my eye. For an instant, I thought someone's house had caught fire. Then I remembered the tree.

As I approached it, I slowed to a walk. There was nothing remarkable about the shape of the tree. A medium-sized maple. But Mrs. Gargan had been right about its colors. Like the messy whirl of an artist's palette, the tree blazed a bright crimson on its lower branches, burned with vivid yellows and oranges in its center, and simmered to deep red at its top. Through these fiery colors were pale-green leaves, as yet untouched by autumn.

Edging closer — like a pilgrim approaching a shrine — I noticed several bare branches near the top, their black twigs scratching the air like claws. The leaves they had shed lay like a scarlet carpet around the trunk.

With its varied nations of color this tree seemed to become a globe embracing in its broad branches all seasons and continents: the spring and summer of the Southern hemisphere in the light and dark greens, the autumn and winter of the Northern in the blazing yellows and bare branches.

As I marveled at this all-encompassing beauty, I thought of Ralph Waldo Emerson's comments about the stars. If the constellations appeared only once in a thousand years, he observed in *Nature*, imagine what an exciting event it would be. But because they're up there every night , we barely give them a look.

I felt the same way about the tree. Because its majesty will last only a week, it should be especially precious to us. And I had almost missed it.

Once in the 19th century when a man noticed a brilliant display of northern lights in the sky over Massachusetts, he tolled a church bell to alert townspeople. That's what I felt like doing about the tree. I wanted to awaken the countryside to its wonder.

I didn't have a church bell, but as I walked home, I did ask each neighbor I passed the same simple but momentous question Mrs. Gargan had asked me: "Have you seen the tree?"

1 Comprehension work

A Read the text again and discuss the following questions.

1. What did the writer learn about the tree from his neighbor?
2. What was the shape of the tree? What were the colors at the lower part, the center and the top of the tree?
3. What did the writer associate these varied colors with?
4. How did Emerson comment on the stars? What was the significance of his comment in relation to the tree?
5. Why should the tree be especially precious to the local people?
6. What did the writer feel like doing at the moment?

7. What does the story want to tell the readers?

B Activity

Suppose you are one of the drivers who has driven past the beautiful tree. Now, you want to tell your friends about its beauty. First fill out the chart, and then prepare a short talk of about one minute.

What made you notice the tree?	How did you find the tree upon a close look?	What associations did the tree awaken in your mind?

2 ▶ Language work

A Fill in the following blanks with the words from the text.

1. During the national holidays, the whole city _____ with flags and flowers.
2. The thick atmosphere which _____ the earth can retain the heat from the sun.
3. As a Holy City, Jerusalem is visited by thousands of _____ every year.
4. The first human landing on the moon is a _____ event in outer space exploration.
5. Men keep dogs as pets for _____ reasons and motives.
6. The children felt dazzled at the _____ brightness of flames.
7. Some animals are not very active during the daytime. You can only see them in _____ at the forests.
8. On reaching the peak, the mountain climbers were amazed at the breathtaking _____ of the view they beheld.

B Rewrite the following sentences with the expressions in the box.

edge	marvel at	jog	swim with
awaken ... to ...	simmer	feel like	

1. The Prime Minister's speech made the nation aware of the imminent danger of the war.

   _____

2. After the examinations, the boy felt the urge to light a fire with all his books and files.

   _____

3. The applicant went into the interview room, his heart full of uncertainty.

   _____

4. The early settlers and travellers were amazed at the abundant land and riches in North America.

   _____

5. The dispute between the two tribes steadily developed into intense hatred.

   _____

6. The policemen moved slowly and cautiously toward the house occupied by gangsters.

   _____

7. Running slowly in the morning for 30 minutes is a good exercise for middle-aged people.

   _____

C Word study.

   a. Give the meanings of the following words or expressions used in the text. You may use an English-English Dictionary. Then give a sentence to illustrate their meanings and usage.

   1. catch one's eyes

      _____

   2. approach

      _____

   3. give ... a look

      _____

   4. alert

      _____

   5. awaken ... to

      _____

   b. Each of the following clues has an example sentence. Use the prompts to produce other sentences with the same pattern as the example.

   1. Prompt: I / jog / bright orange / catch my eyes
      Example: I was jogging down the street when a splash of bright orange caught my eyes.
      a. she / about to leave / purse / catch her eyes
      b. attractive design / garden / villa / catch the woman's eyes
      c. colorful / easily / catch a kid's eyes

   2. Prompt: as / I / approach it / slow to a walk
      Example: As I approached it, I slowed to a walk.
      a. when / soldiers / approach / the top of the mountain / find / enemy / gone
      b. as / deadline / approach / everyone / quicken pace in work
      c. cat / approach / bird / before / prance upon it

   3. Prompt: because / they / are there / we / give a look
      Example: Because they're up there every night, we barely give them a look.
      a. Mr. White / going to / move / give his house a look
      b. as / mouse / so insignificant / lion / barely give a look
      c. little girl / huddle / in the corner / passers-by / give a look

   4. Prompt: a man / notice / northern lights / he / alert / townspeople

Example: When a man noticed a brilliant display of northern lights in the sky over Massachusetts, he tolled a church bell to alert townspeople.

   a. old man / discover / enemy ring / bell / alert / villagers

   b. driver / press / horn / alert / cyclist

   c. siren / sound / alert / people / air attacks

5. Prompt: I / awaken ... to / wonder

   Example: I wanted to awaken the countryside to its wonder.

   a. she / write / columns / awaken ... to / corruption

   b. raining / a week / we / must / awaken ... to / floods

   c. words / at last / awaken ... to / responsibility as a father

PART 3 Extended Activities

1 Dictation

2 Read more

Leaf Magic

I can't take a fall walk without thinking about the gentle miracle of the leaf. During the summer when sunlight strikes a leaf, and water is drawn up from the tree's roots, and carbon dioxide is sucked out of the air, an amazing green substance in the leaf is busy making us food and giving us oxygen. Without chlorophyll, we would die.

In the fall, when the days shorten and grow colder, leaves simply stop producing this life-giving material. They are orchestrating their own death, for the sake of the plant's survival. That's why leaves turn yellow and orange. The yellow xanthophyll and the orange and red carotenes have been there all along. They've just been obscured by the green chlorophyll.

We would have yellow and orange leaves any fall, regardless of the weather. But it's the brilliant reds and scarlets that depend upon a set of weather conditions as precise and balanced as a Bach fugue. If we get nice warm fall days with intense sun, leaves manufacture a lot of sugar, which helps produce a red pigment called anthocyanin. If these warm days are followed by warm nights, those gorgeous reds are simply sent downward, in the form of sugars, for winter food storage. But if the nights are chilly, the sugar doesn't move. It's trapped in the leaves and the anthocyanin accumulates — the roots lose out a little, but we get to feast our eyes.

Which brings me to my basic question: does knowing all this, or any of it, improve a walk in the fall?

I used to answer with a resounding no, feeling that facts interfered with esthetics. But that was back in my Dark Ages. With the dawning of science — and believe me, in my mind, it's just a little sliver of light — I not only look more, I see more. A bit of knowledge scattered along a fall trail can intensify its pleasures.

But now I see things differently. I think knowing about the natural world has more to do with the desire to belong to it, rather than own it. There's a kind of comfortable pleasure in sitting on a tree stump in the fall and recognizing the bittersweet, honeysuckle, and wild grape.

My favorite fall tree is the sugar maple — because I climbed one as a kid. I would no more confuse a sugar maple with a silver maple than I would my sister with someone else — because, as a child, I sat for so long on a wide branch particularly suitable for reading Nancy Drew.

As I climbed the steep hill from the beach that day, I stopped to catch my breath, and to admire the first faint changing colors. And I could see where all these living things lead: down the path and through the woods and cross the water, and who knows, to other continents and other forests, where leaves and plants are doing nature's business — and just as a sideline, really, giving us life.

Notes

1. fall: autumn (American English)
2. chlorophyll /'kɒrəfɪl/: 叶绿素
3. xanthophyll /'zænθəfɪl/: 叶黄素
4. carotene /'kærətiːn/: 胡萝卜素
5. Bach: Johann Sebastian Bach (1685 – 1750), a German musician and composer, one of the best known and most admired of all time, well-known for his organ music. (巴赫)
6. fugue /fjuːg/: 赋格曲
7. anthocyanin /ˌænθəˈsaɪnɪn/: 花青素
8. Dark Ages: the period in European history from AD 476 (the fall of Rome) to about AD 1000. It is generally regarded as a time when society was not very developed in art, education, literature, etc. The writer is using the term metaphorically to mean that many years ago she did not have the scientific knowledge about the changing colors of the tree leaves.
9. honeysuckle: 金银花
10. Nancy Drew: a character in children's stories who is a detective and finds answers to mysteries. These popular stories are written by Carolyn Keene, an American writer.

A True / False / Not Mentioned (NM).
1. Leaves can produce food for people.
2. Leaves turn yellow for the sake of their own survival.
3. The xanthophyll and carotenes only exist in leaves in the fall.
4. The chlorophyll is the substance that turns leaves into yellow and orange.
5. Bach loved autumn leaves.
6. The brilliant red and scarlet of autumn leaves appear only if the warm days are followed by warm nights.
7. In the author's opinion, facts never interfere with esthetics.
8. A bit of knowledge about leaves helps the author enjoy the magic of leaves more.
9. If you add knowledge to your mental store, you add more happiness to your life.

B Topics for discussion.
1. What are the necessary weather conditions for the brilliant red and scarlet leaves?
2. What is the author's opinion about the relationship between knowledge and aesthetics? And what is your opinion?
3. Which season brings out the best view in a year? Give your reasons.

3 Grammar work

Mark the mistakes in the following sentences.
1. I can't swim. — I can't neither.
2. When I was young, my father was often used to take me to the museum on Sundays.
3. He was elected the chairman of the committee.
4. You will get an electric shock if you touch that wire — it's alive!
5. The police banned us to negotiate individually with the kidnapper.
6. He persuaded us to go with him to the party on Friday evening, but none of us listened!
7. I'm quite exciting about the possibilities of visiting the United States.
8. The timetable will not remain in operation until the new scheme is put into use.
9. He doesn't seem to understand our position. So there is no point to argue with him.
10. According to my opinion, two-thirds of the students don't like the mid-term examination.

4 Word formation

It's a <u>medium-sized</u> maple.

Supply the compound adjectives according to the example.
*example: **having dark skin** **<u>dark-skinned</u>***
1. having long legs _____
2. having white hair _____
3. having a round face _____
4. without pity, cruel _____

5. having a readiness to become angry quickly and easily _____

6. able to think quickly, intelligent _____

7. being in low spirits _____

8. showing unwillingness to accept different ideas _____

> *Adj + n + ed* — a way to form compound adjectives, for example, medium-sized, black-haired, dark-skinned. There is a hyphen (-) between the first and second word, and a suffix *-ed* is added after the second word.

5 ▷ Vocabulary work

Fill in each blank with the verb in its proper form.

1. All the books and magazines on the shelves ought to _____ (read) inside the reading room.

2. The meeting of the company board is going to _____ (hold) tomorrow.

3. Laptops used to _____ (regard) as a symbol of social status.

4. You have to _____ (submit) your paper by the end of this month.

5. The traffic rules mustn't _____ (violate).

6. The questions may _____ (answer) in short form.

7. Owing to bad weather, the college sports meeting has to _____ (postpone).

8. Matches should _____ (keep) where children can't get them.

9. He _____ (wake) by the noise from the next room.

10. I can't help _____ (admire) the amazing pink of the peach trees in bloom.

6 ▷ Translation

Put the following sentences into English.

1. 卫生间满地是水。**swim with**

2. 在那一瞬间我认为我要输了。**for an instant**

3. 我在街上走着，突然一张海报引起了我的注意。**catch somebody's eye**

4. 一个小村庄坐落在这恬静的山谷里。**lie**

5. 外面空气多清新，如果你喜欢的话，我们出去走走。**feel like**

6. 他老是干扰我们的计划。**interfere with**

7. 由于机械故障，他们在电梯里面困了两个小时。**trap**

7 ▷ Writing

A Describing shades of colors.

Here are three ways to describe shades of colors:

* use *light* or *dark*, *bright* or *dull* before words of color to describe its different shade, e.g.

light green, dull blue

- use the suffix *-ish*, e.g. bluish = slightly blue
- use the *-ish* word before another color word to describe a combination of two or more colors, e.g. brownish yellow

Describe the colors of five objects. Pay attention to their shades.

Example: The cover of the book is brownish red.

1. (your school building) _____
2. (the meadow in your college garden) _____
3. (your English teacher's dress / coat) _____
4. (your favorite color) _____
5. (the furniture in your bedroom) _____

B Write a short paragraph describing your school garden in autumn.

Our School Garden in Autumn

C ultural Information

Read the passage below, and then complete the task of cultural study.

Traditional Western Wedding

Before the Wedding Ceremony

In the traditional wedding ceremony, the bridegroom is not supposed to see the bride on the day of the wedding until they meet in church as this is considered to be bad luck.

The bridegroom arrives at the church first and waits inside, near the altar with the best man.

The families of the bride and bridegroom, and the wedding guests, sit in rows in the church.

Just before the wedding ceremony begins, the bride arrives at the church in a car with her father. It is usually an expensive car, such as a Rolls Royce or a limousine, hired for the occasion and decorated with ribbons. There are often jokes made about the bride arriving late at the church.

The Ceremony

It is the custom for the bride's father to "give her away" (officially to "give her to the bridegroom"). The bride and her father walk slowly up the aisle of the church, with the bridesmaids. People sometimes talk about "walking up the aisle" when they mean "getting married". When the bride and bridegroom are together at the altar, the priest or minister begins the wedding service. The words that are said during the wedding service are well known to most people. During the service, the bridegroom gives the bride a wedding ring (a plain gold ring) and says "With this ring I thee wed" ("With this ring I marry you"). Sometimes the bride also gives a ring to the bridegroom. The priest or minister asks the bride and bridegroom in turn: "Will you have this man / woman to be your wedded husband / wife?" The bride and bridegroom each say "I will". At the end of the ceremony, the priest or minister says: "I pronounce you man and wife", which means that they are officially married. The bride and bridegroom then sign the register (a special book which is the official record of their marriage).

After the Ceremony

Outside the church, the friends of the bride and bridegroom throw confetti (small pieces of colored paper) or rice over them. Photographs are usually taken of the bride and bridegroom and their families and friends.

When the wedding pictures have been taken, there will be a wedding reception, which is a special meal (wedding breakfast) and party to celebrate the wedding. During the meal the bride and bridegroom cut the wedding cake and give it to their guests. At the end of the meal there are speeches, usually made by the bride's father, the bridegroom and the best man. It is traditional for the best man to make a speech in which he talks about funny and embarrassing things that happened to the bridegroom in the past.

Before the reception ends, the bride and bridegroom usually drive away to a hotel to spend their wedding night before beginning their honeymoon. Their car is usually decorated by their friends. There is often a sign saying "just married" and sometimes tin cans are tied to the back of the car. Before she leaves, the bride throws her bouquet to her friends to catch. According to custom, anyone who catches it will be the next one to get married.

 Cultural Study Task

What is the wedding ceremony like in your place? How are they different from the western traditions? Are there any special sayings, or expressions in relation to marriage in your culture? Write a mini-essay describing the marriage ceremony in your culture.

One of These Days

Introduction

In this unit, you will learn to use English for

▌ Talking about Latin American writer Gabriel García Márquez

▌ Turning narrative into conversation and drama

▌ Reading short stories and writing literary analysis

PART 1 Communicative Activities

1 ▶ Interactive listening and speaking

A Listening

In this part, you will listen to an audio clip of a lecture given by a professor of Latin

American literature on the early life of Gabriel García Márquez. Listen and complete the task below.

1. When and where was Gabriel Garcia Marquez born?
   a. He was born in 1928 in a small town in Colombia.
   b. He was born in 1938 in a small town in Colombia.
   c. He was born in 1928 in a small town in Columbia.

2. His early life was greatly influenced by _____.
   a. His great grandparents and his own parents
   b. His grandparents on his mother's side, and his own parents
   c. His grandparents on his father's side, and his own parents

3. His grandfather was _____ when he was young.
   a. a banana farmer and political activist
   b. a police officer who killed someone once
   c. a military officer and political activist

4. Which of the following statements is true according to the recording?
   a. His grandmother had less influence than her husband on young Gabriel García Márquez.
   b. His grandmother knew many more stories than her husband did.
   c. His grandmother had as great influence as her husband on young Gabriel García Márquez.

5. Which of the following statements is NOT true about Márquez's parents?
   a. His grandparents disliked his father, but later changed their mind.
   b. His mother disliked his father at the beginning.
   c. His father disliked his mother at the beginning, but later he changed his mind.

6. Which of the following life experiences can be found in his novels *Hundred Years of Solitude* and *Love in the Time of Cholera*?
   a. The stories his grandfather told can be found in the first story, not in the second story.
   b. The story about his parents' marriage can be found in the second story, but not in the first one.
   c. The stories told by his grandmother can be found in the first story, and the story of his parents' marriage in the second.

B Discussion

Listen, and take notes. Discuss these questions with your partner. Then complete the tasks.

The professor briefly sketched the four people in Márquez's early life.

What kind of persons are the four people like (grandfather, grandmother, mother, and father)? Give enough details to sketch their personalities.

You may write your description in the table below.

People in Márquez's early life	Sketch
His grandfather	
His grandmother	
His mother	
His father	

2 ▶ Role-play

Read the following excerpts, and work in small groups to turn them into a dialog for excerpt 1, and a short play for excerpt 2.

Excerpt 1

Turn this excerpt into a dialog between Young Gabriel and his grandfather.

His grandfather once said to young Gabriel, "Don't listen to that. Those are women's beliefs." And yet listen he did, for his grandmother had a unique way of telling stories. No matter how fantastic or unbelievable her stories were, she always delivered them as if they were the truth. It was a deadpan style that, some thirty years later, her grandson adopted for his greatest novel *Hundred Years of Solitude*.

Excerpt 2

Turn this excerpt into a short play.

Characters:
Grandfather
Grandmother
Their daughter
Her young suitor, a former medical student

She was a spirited girl, but unfortunately fell in love with a man named Gabriel Eligio García. "Unfortunately," for García was disliked by her parents. Among other things, García had a reputation as a philanderer, the father of four illegitimate children. He was not exactly the man the Colonel had envisioned who should have won the heart of his daughter — and yet he did, wooing her with violin serenades, love poems, countless letters — and even telegraph messages. They tried all they could to get rid of the man, but he kept coming back, and it was obvious that their daughter was committed to him. Finally they surrendered to his romantic tenacity, and the Colonel gave her hand in marriage to the former medical student.

3 ▶ Learning phrases

Explain these terms.

1. maternal grandparents _____

   Then, who are one's patriarchal /ˌpeɪtrɪˈɑrkəl/ parents? _____

2. illegitimate children _____

3. spirited girl _____

4. win the heart of sb _____

5. deliver the story in a deadpan style _____

6. father over 16 children _____

7. envision him as someone to win the heart of their daughter _____

8. surrender to his romantic tenacity _____

9. give her hand to sb _____

10. sb has a reputation as a philanderer _____

● Proverb

Great minds think alike.

PART 2 Reading and Language Activities

Text   One of These Days   By Gabriel García Márquez

▶ Pre-reading tasks **Discuss the following questions.**

How would you feel if a dentist pulls out a tooth from a patient without using anesthesia? And why does he want to do so?

► Read the text

Monday dawned warm and rainless. Aurelio Escovar, a dentist without a degree, and a very early riser, opened his office at six. He took some false teeth, still mounted in their plaster mold, out of the glass case and put on the table a fistful of instruments which he arranged in size order, as if they were on display. He wore a collarless striped shirt, closed at the neck with a golden stud, and pants held up by suspenders. He was erect and skinny, with a look that rarely corresponded to the situation, the way deaf people have of looking.

When he had things arranged on the table, he pulled the drill toward the dental chair and sat down to polish the false teeth. He seemed not to be thinking about what he was doing, but worked steadily, pumping the drill with his feet, even when he didn't need it.

After eight he stopped for a while to look at the sky through the window, and he saw two pensive buzzards who were drying themselves in the sun on the ridgepole of the house next door. He went on working with the idea that before lunch it would rain again. The shrill voice of his eleven-year-old son interrupted his concentration.

"Papa."

"What?"

"The Mayor wants to know if you'll pull his tooth."

"Tell him I'm not here."

He was polishing a gold tooth. He held it at arm's length, and examined it with his eyes half closed. His son shouted again from the little waiting room.

"He says you are, too, because he can hear you."

The dentist kept examining the tooth. Only when he had put it on the table with the finished work did he say: "So much the better."

He operated the drill again. He took several pieces of a bridge out of a cardboard box where he kept the things he still had to do and began to polish the gold.

"Papa."

"What?"

He still hadn't changed his expression.

"He says if you don't take out his tooth, he'll shoot you."

Without hurrying, with an extremely tranquil movement, he stopped pedaling the drill, pushed it away from the chair, and pulled the lower drawer of the table all the way out. There was a revolver. "OK," he said. "Tell him to come and shoot me."

He rolled the chair over opposite the door, his hand resting on the edge of the drawer. The Mayor appeared at the door. He had shaved the left side of his face, but the other side, swollen and in pain, had a five-day-old beard. The dentist saw many nights of desperation in his dull eyes. He closed the drawer with his fingertips and said softly: "Sit down."

"Good morning," said the Mayor.

"Morning," said the dentist.

While the instruments were boiling, the Mayor leaned his skull on the headrest of the chair and felt better. His breath was icy. It was a poor office: an old wooden chair, the pedal drill, a glass case with ceramic bottles. Opposite the chair was a window with a shoulder-high cloth curtain. When he felt the dentist approach, the Mayor braced his heels and opened his mouth.

Aurelio Escovar turned his head toward the light. After inspecting the infected tooth, he closed the Mayor's jaw with a cautious pressure of his fingers.

"It has to be without anesthesia," he said.

"Why?"

"Because you have an abscess."

The Mayor looked him in the eye. "All right," he said, and tried to smile. The dentist did not return the smile. He brought the basin of sterilized instruments to the worktable and took them out of the water with a pair of cold tweezers, still without hurrying. Then he pushed the spittoon with the tip of his shoe, and went to wash his hands in the washbasin. He did all this without looking at the Mayor. But the Mayor didn't take his eyes off him.

It was a lower wisdom tooth. The dentist spread his feet and grasped the tooth with the hot forceps. The Mayor seized the arms of the chair, braced his feet with all his strength, and felt an icy void in his kidneys, but didn't make a sound. The dentist moved only his wrist. Without rancor, rather with a bitter tenderness, he said:

"Now you'll pay for our twenty dead men."

The Mayor felt the crunch of bones in his jaw, and his eyes filled with tears. But he didn't breathe until he felt the tooth come out. Then he saw it through his tears. It seemed so foreign to his pain that he failed to understand his torture of the five previous nights.

Bent over the spittoon, sweating, panting, he unbuttoned his tunic and reached for the handkerchief in his pants pocket. The dentist gave him a clean cloth.

"Dry your tears," he said.

The Mayor did. He was trembling. While the dentist washed his hands, he saw the crumbling ceiling and a dusty spider web with spider's eggs and dead insects. The dentist

Notes

1 About the author: Gabriel García Márquez is not only famous for his 1982 Nobel Prize, he is also known for criticizing corrupted politics in Colombia. This is one of his short stories of social criticism.

2 Aurelio Escovar /ˌɔreɪˈlɪəʊ ˌeʃkəʊˈvar/ (Spanish personal name)

3 anesthesia /ˌænəsˈðiːʒə/ loss of sensation of pains by using medicine

4 abscess /ˈæbˌses/ a localized collection of pus surrounded by inflamed tissue

5 braced his feet: placed his feet against something as if in suffering from pains or intense worries

6 crunch of bones: (metaphorically) loud crushing sound of bones breaking

7 gargle: clean one's mouth or throat by moving water inside it, and then spit it out

returned, drying his hands. "Go to bed," he said, "and gargle with salt water." The Mayor stood up, said goodbye with a casual military salute, and walked toward the door, stretching his legs, without buttoning up his tunic.

"Send the bill," he said.

"To you or the town?"

The Mayor didn't look at him. He closed the door and said through the screen: "It's the same damn thing."

Comprehension work

A Discussion

1. What is the story about? Select one of the suggestions below, and argue for position by using details from the story.
   a. Revenge
   b. Medical malpractice
   c. Punishment
   d. Political corruption
   e. Dire conditions of dental services
   f. Power

2. Why did Escovar despise the Mayor so much?

3. Why did not Escovar use anesthesia when he pulled the infected tooth for the Mayor? Was it out of sound medical reasons, negligence, or malignity?

4. What does the mayor mean by "It's the same damn thing"?

B Analysis

The story has clearly moved through three stages in the relationship of the power balance between the mayor and Escovar. Study the story in pairs and complete the table below.

Stages	Power balance *Evidence*
1	The mayor is more powerful than Escovar.
2	The mayor is less powerful than Escovar.

3	The mayor resumes his power.
	What does this change tell us?

C Cloze

Fill in the blanks with suitable words.

Aurelio Escovar is introduced as a poor dentist without a (1) _____. He is busy polishing false teeth early one morning when the mayor arrives to see him. At first he (2) _____ to see this would-be patient, until the mayor, who has been suffering severe toothache for five days and is desperate, threatens to (3) _____ him. Eventually the dentist lets him in, examines him, and then removes the (4) _____ wisdom tooth, without anesthesia.

Readers can find out that the dentist has (5) _____ made the mayor suffer all this time, and he gives the reason as he pulls out the tooth, saying "Now you'll pay for our twenty dead men." When the mayor has recovered and wiped his tears, he leaves, telling the dentist to send the bill. When Escovar asks where to send the (6) _____, "To you or the town?," the mayor replies, "It's the same damn thing."

Marquez captures the peculiar nature of medical (or in this case dental) power in this tale of manipulation. Escovar the dentist is not a (7) _____ man in this town; he is not wealthy and his office is poorly (8) _____ and dirty. The mayor is the epitome of apparently corrupt, even murderous, political power. But the infection entirely (9) _____ this hierarchy, placing the mayor at the dentist's mercy.

The power is profound, but temporary, for as soon as Escovar has removed the tooth, the mayor is released from him — looking at the (10) _____ tooth, the mayor "failed to understand his (11) _____ of the five previous nights" — and when he leaves, the mayor reiterates that he and the town are "the same thing," that his power extends beyond himself.

No matter how (12) _____ it is, Escovar succeeded in demonstrating that professional knowledge or skills, in the face of social oppression, can be an effective tool for revenge in "one of these days".

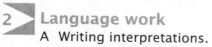

2 ▶ Language work

A Writing interpretations.

Rewrite the following sentences in your own words to bring about the major features of the description of the character, or make the meaning of the sentence easier to understand.

1. What does the dentist look like? What kind of air does he usually assume?
   He wore a collarless striped shirt, closed at the neck with a golden stud, and pants held up by suspenders. He was erect and skinny, with a look that rarely corresponded to the situation, the way deaf people have of looking.
   Rewrite:

   _____

   _____

2. Explain what Escovar meant when he said "So much the better".
   Rewrite:

   _____

   _____

3. Read this description, and describe what the two characters might be thinking now.
   The Mayor looked him in the eye. "All right," he said, and tried to smile. The dentist did not return the smile. He brought the basin of sterilized instruments to the worktable and took them out of the water with a pair of cold tweezers, still without hurrying. Then he pushed the spittoon with the tip of his shoe, and went to wash his hands in the washbasin. He did all this without looking at the Mayor. But the Mayor didn't take his eyes off him.
   Rewriting:

   _____

   _____

4. Even though the mayor was at the mercy of Escovar on the dental chair, he seemed to be a tough guy too. Describe the scene of his suffering in your own words.
   The Mayor felt the crunch of bones in his jaw, and his eyes filled with tears. But he didn't breathe until he felt the tooth come out. Then he saw it through his tears. It seemed so foreign to his pain that he failed to understand his torture of the five previous nights.
   Rewriting:

   _____

   _____

B Word study.

Read the following sentences using the phrases in relation to "dawn". Fill in appropriate words to complete the sentences.

1. It began to **dawn** _____ her that she was lost.
2. She drove _____ **dawn** till dusk for a whole day, and was utterly exhausted.
3. The invention of steam engines _____ the **dawn** of modern era.
4. People have fought with each other _____ the **dawn** of history.

5. These animals mostly hunt _____ **dawn** and dusk, and sleep in the morning, afternoon, and night.

6. The dentist was an early riser, usually got up at the _____ of **dawn**.

PART 3 Extended Activities

1 Dictation

2 Read more

Read the story, and answer the questions below.

What is the difference between shopping for one and shopping for a family? Have you noticed them at the checking out counter in a supermarket? Have you also heard snaps of conversation there too?

Shopping for One
By Anne Cassidy

"So what did you say?" Jean heard the blonde woman in front of her talking to her friend.

"Well," the darker woman began, "I said I'm not having that woman there. I don't see why I should. I mean I'm not being old fashioned but I don't see why I should have to put up with her at family occasions. After all ... " Jean noticed the other woman giving an accompaniment of nods and handshaking at the appropriate parts. They fell into silence and the queue moved forward a couple of steps.

Jean felt her patience beginning to itch. Looking into her wire basket she counted ten items. That meant she couldn't go through the quick till but simply had to wait behind elephantine shopping loads; giant bottles of coke crammed in beside twenty-pound bags of potatoes and "Special offer" drums of bleach. Somewhere at the bottom, Jean thought, there was always a plastic carton of eggs or a see-through tray of tomatoes which fell casualty to the rest. There was nothing else for it – she'd just have to wait.

"After all," the dark woman resumed her conversation, "how would it look if she was there when I turned up?" Her friend shook her head slowly from side to side and ended with a quick nod.

Should she have got such a small size salad cream? Jean wasn't sure. She was sick of throwing away half-used bottles of stuff.

"He came back to you after all," the blonde woman suddenly said. Jean looked up quickly and immediately felt her cheeks flush. She bent over and began to rearrange the items in her shopping basket.

"On his hands and knees," the dark woman spoke in a triumphant voice. "Begged me take him back."

She gritted her teeth together. Should she go and change it for a larger size? Jean looked behind and saw that she was hemmed in by three large trolleys. She'd lose her place in the queue. There was something so pitiful about buying small sizes of everything. It was as though everyone knew.

"You can always tell a person by their shopping," was one of her mother's favorite maxims. She looked into the shopping basket: individual fruit pies, small salad cream, yogurt, tomatoes, cat food and a chicken quarter.

"It was only for sex you know. He admitted as much to me when he came back," the dark woman informed her friend. Her friend began to load her shopping on to the conveyor belt. The cashier, doing what looked like an in-depth study of a biro, suddenly said, "Make it out to J. Sainsbury PLC." She was addressing a man who had been poised and waiting to write out a check for a few moments. His wife was loading what looked like a gross of fish fingers into a cardboard box marked "Whiskas". It was called a division of labor.

Jean looked again at her basket and began to feel the familiar feeling of regret that visited her from time to time. Hemmed in between family-size cartons of cornflakes and giant packets of washing-powder, her individual yogurt seemed to say it all. She looked up towards a plastic bookstand which stood beside

Notes

1. About the author: Anne Cassidy, British writer, born in London in 1952. The story was first published in 1984.
2. quick till: (British English) checking out counter
3. drums of bleach: large cans of liquid for washing
4. biro: a ballpoint pen
5. Make it out to J. Sainsburg PLC: Write your check payable to J. Sainsburg PLC.
6. Marks and Spencer carrier bag: the shopping bag of Marks and Spencer
7. starters orders: waiting for someone to give the order to start moving ahead
8. a non conformer: someone who doesn't conform to the tradition
9. half a consumer unit half a family, wife or husband in this case
10. tea: british English, meal

the till. A slim glossy hardback caught her eye. The words *Cooking for One* screamed out from the front cover. Think of all the oriental foods you can get into, her friend had said. He was so traditional after all. Nodding in agreement with her thoughts Jean found herself eye to eye with the blonde woman, who, obviously not prepared to tolerate nodding at anyone else, gave her a blank, hard look and handed her what looked like a black plastic ruler with the words "Next customer please" printed on it in bold letters. She turned back to her friend. Jean put the ruler down on the conveyor belt.

She thought about their shopping trips, before, when they were together, which for some reason seemed to assume massive proportions considering there were only two of them. All that rushing round, he pushing the trolley dejectedly, she firing questions at him. Salmon? Toilet rolls? Coffee? Peas? She remembered he only liked the processed kind. It was all such a performance. Standing there holding her wire basket, embarrassed by its very emptiness, was like something out of a soap opera.

"Of course, we've had our ups and downs," the dark woman continued, lazily passing a few items down to her friend who was now on to what looked like her fourth Marks and Spencer carrier bag.

Jean began to load her food on to the conveyor belt. She picked up the cookery book and felt the frustrations of indecision. It was only ninety pence but it seemed to define everything, to pinpoint her aloneness, to prescribe an empty future. She put it back in its place.

"So that's why I couldn't have her there you see," the dark woman was summing up. She lowered her voice to a loud whisper which immediately alerted a larger audience. "And anyway, when he settles back in, I'm sure we'll sort out the other business then." The friends exchanged knowing expressions and the blonde woman got her purse out of a neat leather bag. She peeled off three ten pound notes and handed them to the cashier.

Jean opened her carrier bag ready for her shopping. She turned to watch the two women as they walked off, the blond pushing the trolley and the other seemingly carrying on with her story.

The cashier was looking expectantly at her and Jean realized that she had totaled up. It was four pounds and eighty-seven pence. She had the right money, it just meant sorting her change out. She had an inclination that the people behind her were becoming impatient. She noticed their stack of items all lined and waiting, it seemed, for starters orders. Brown bread and peppers, olive oil and lentils and, in the center, a stray packet of beef burgers.

She gave over her money and picked up her carrier bag. She felt a sense of relief to be away from the mass of people. She felt out of place, a non conformer, half a consumer unit.

Walking out of the door she wondered what she might have for tea. Possibly chicken, she thought, with salad. Walking towards her car she thought that she should have bought the cookery book after all. She suddenly felt much better in the fresh air. She'd buy it next week. And in future she'd buy a large salad cream. After all, what if people came round unexpectedly?

Choose the best answer to each of the following questions.

1. Why did Jean feel that her patience began to itch?
   A. Several customers had large loads on their shopping trolley.
   B. She wasn't comfortable to eves-drop the conversation between two intimate women friends.
   C. Both A and B.
   D. She had nothing to amuse herself in the queue for checking out.

2. Why did Jean suddenly feel the need to rearrange the items in her shopping basket?
   A. She found her times in her basket were not properly placed.
   B. She was embarrassed at hearing the snaps of conversation, so she was trying to divert her attention to something else.
   C. She wanted to check out if the items were correct in her basket.
   D. She felt the salad cream was too small in size.

3. What do Jean's shopping items tell the reader about her?
   A. She may have separated from her boyfriend, and now lived alone.
   B. She may be a career woman, single, having no boyfriend.
   C. Either A or B is possible.
   D. She is divorced, and now lives alone.

4. How did Jean feel about her life when she put back the cookery book?
   A. She felt desperate for companionship.
   B. She felt a little depressed about her future.
   C. She felt satisfied about living alone.
   D. She didn't know how to arrange her future life.

5. The author describes in the end that she felt "out of place, a non conformer, half a consumer unit". What does this description tell us about Jean?
   A. She felt that she had been to a wrong supermarket.
   B. She felt that traditional views did not encourage a woman to live alone.
   C. She bought too little, as half a consumer unit, making little contribution to society.
   D. She was sad that she had to live alone.

6. Why did she make up her mind that she would buy a larger salad cream in the future?
   A. She was thinking of entertaining her guests in the future.
   B. She longed for companionship.
   C. She longed for friendship.
   D. She longed to marry again in the future.

7. What do you know about the darker woman and the blonde woman through snaps of their conversation?
   A. The darker woman had a boyfriend, but their relationship was unsteady.
   B. The blonde woman had a boyfriend, but their relationship wasn't steady.
   C. The darker woman was married, but she had some trouble now with her husband.

D. The blonde woman listened to the darker woman's story, and tried to help her to solve the problem.

8. Which sentence in this short story makes Jean's feelings and judgements sound credible to the reader?

A. She thought about their shopping trips, before, when they were together, which for some reason seemed to assume massive proportions considering there were only two of them.

B. Somewhere at the bottom, Jean thought, there was always a plastic carton of eggs or a see-through tray of tomatoes which fell casualty to the rest.

C. And in future she'd buy a large salad cream. After all, what if people came round unexpectedly?

D. "You can always tell a person by their shopping," was one of her mother's favorite maxims.

 3 Grammar work

Correct the mistakes in the following sentences.

1. Look out for the traffic sign. — Which traffic sign do I have to look out?
2. I've borrowed some money. — Who did you borrow it?
3. There are two film stars at a table behind you. — Which table are they sitting?
4. There is a big box to pack all the clothes.
5. Have you got a pen to sign these papers?
6. Is there a room to hang our coats?
7. I prefer my new school to the one I went before.
8. What's this? — A small gift for you to remember us.
9. Turn on the radio, will you? — Which program do you want to listen?
10. They are the people we should learn, aren't they?

 4 Word formation

Fill in the following blanks with derivatives of the words in brackets.

1. This answer is _____ (correct), which means you lose a point.
2. An advertising supplement is issued _____ (regularly) with the newspaper.
3. There is a great deal of _____ (decide) about how to deal with the problem.
4. It is _____ (legal) to drive a car without a driving licence.
5. Now that John has got a job he is financially _____ (depend).
6. The disabled do not mean to be _____ (able).
7. They read nothing and they know nothing — they're completely _____ (literate).
8. Your _____ (ability) to use a computer could be a serious disadvantage if you apply for this job.

in- (also *il-*, *im-*, *ir-*) — a prefix used with adjectives, adverbs and nouns, meaning "not," e.g. injustice, illogical, immorally, irrelevance, etc.

5 Vocabulary work

Fill in the blanks with appropriate words.

| scornful | superior | laughter | scream |
| sigh | light up | awful | hurt |

1. You always seem so _____, as if you thought other people had nothing important to say.
2. She arrived in a beautiful new car and was very _____ of my old bicycle.
3. I'm sorry you feel so _____; but there really is no need to cry.
4. "I feel regretful that I never took up the opportunity to go to university," he said with a deep _____.
5. They were a happy group of people: you could always hear _____ coming from their house.
6. The little girl _____ for help when she saw a mouse under her chair.
7. Their eyes _____ when they saw the film star.
8. It was _____ to see him in such pain.

C ultural Information

Read the passage below, and then complete the task of cultural study.

Christopher Columbus and His Discovery of Americas

In the fifteenth century, Europeans had a tremendous zeal for finding a new, shorter route to the riches of Asia. An Italian mariner named Cristoforo Colombo, known in English as Christopher Columbus (1451-1506), proposed sailing to the markets of Asia by a western route. On the basis of wide reading of literature on geography, Columbus believed (mistakenly, of course) that Japan should be less than 2 500 nautical miles west of the Canary Islands. This geography suggested that sailing west from Europe to Asian markets would be profitable, and Columbus sought royal sponsorship for a voyage to prove his ideas. The Portuguese court declined his proposal, skeptical of his knowledge of geography.

Eventually Fernando and Isabel, King and Queen of Spain, agreed to underwrite Columbus's expedition, and in August 1492 his fleet of three ships departed Palos in southern

Spain. On the morning of 12 October 1492, he made landfall at an island in the Bahamas that the native Taino inhabitants called Guanahani and that Columbus rechristened San Salvador (also known as Watling Island). Thinking that he had arrived in the spice islands known familiarly as the Indies, Columbus called the Tainos "Indians." In search of gold he sailed around the Caribbean for almost three months, and at the large island of Cuba he sent a delegation to seek the court of the emperor of China. When Columbus returned to Spain, he reported to his royal sponsors that he had reached islands just off the coast of Asia.

Columbus never reached the riches of Asia, and despite three additional voyages across the Atlantic Ocean, he obtained very little gold in the Caribbean. Yet news of his voyage spread rapidly throughout Europe, and hundreds of Spanish, English, French, and Dutch mariners soon followed in his wake. Particularly in the early sixteenth century, many of them continued to seek the passage to Asian waters that Columbus himself had pursued. Over a longer term, however, it became clear that the American continents and the Caribbean islands themselves held abundant opportunities for entrepreneurs. Thus Columbus's voyages to the western hemisphere had unintended but momentous consequences, since they established links between the eastern and western hemispheres and paved the way for the conquest, settlement, and exploitation of the Americas by European peoples.

(Based on Bentley, H. J, and Ziegler, F. H. *Traditions Encounters*)

 Cultural Study Task

Zheng He and his seven naval expeditions (1405-1433)
Study the following website, and write a synopsis about Zheng He's naval expeditions during the Ming Dynasty.
(Visit the website: http://library.thinkquest.org / 20176/chengho.htm)

New York City

Introduction

In this unit, you will learn to use English for

▶ Talking about tourist attractions in New York City

▶ Explaining the reasons and arrangements for a tour

▶ Talking about American culture in relation to New York City

PART 1 Communicative Activities

1 ▶ Interactive listening and speaking

A   Pre-listening task.

In this recording, a tour guide is taking you to visit nine tourist attractions in New

York City. **Before you listen, make guesses of the possible places that you will see today.**

Tick your guesses in the list below:

◇ Canal Street
◇ Madison Square Building
◇ Chrysler Building
◇ Natural History Museum
◇ Lincoln Center
◇ Chinatown
◇ Battery Park
◇ Time Square
◇ Ground Zero

◇ Empire State Building
◇ The St. Patrick's Cathedral
◇ Rockefeller Center
◇ Broadway
◇ Little Italy
◇ Wall Street
◇ Ellis Island
◇ Fifth Avenue
◇ The Brooklyn Bridge

B Listening: Sequence.

Now, listen to the audio clip, and put the tourist locations into the correct sequence.

C Listening for details.

Listen again, and describe the major features for these attractions.

No.	Attractions	Major features
1		
2		
3		
4		
5		
6		
7		
8		
9		

2 ▶ Speaking

Form in groups. Select two of the locations that you would like to visit in ONE day. Report your agreed places to the class, and explain why and how you choose them.

No.	The places to see	Reasons
1		
2		

PART 2 Reading and Language Activities

Text   New York City and Its Immigration Culture   By Thomas W. Santos

▶ Pre-reading tasks   **Complete the following tasks.**

Write the facts you know about New York City _____

Write what you hope to know more about it _____

Let's read the text below.

▶ Read the text

In the span of just a few centuries, what is now New York City went from a verdant wilderness on the edge of the known world to a sprawling megalopolis that commands international attention. (1) _____, New Yorkers remain stubbornly sentimental about the city they call home. Painters, writers, and filmmakers have tried to capture its essence and appeal. But nothing compares to actually being there, walking the streets, and soaking in the unique, syncopated rhythm of the city.

(2) _____, New York cannot look back on millennia of development and history. Even so, unprecedented growth and prosperity over a relatively short time has raised New York to the level of the greatest cities of civilization. (3) ___ _____, "The City," as people call it, is a world of commerce, imagination, diversity, and productivity. The city actually consists of five boroughs: Manhattan, Brooklyn, the Bronx, Queens, and Staten Island. Yet, when people speak of New York City, they generally are talking about the island of Manhattan. This is where it started. This is where the vitality of the city is most evident. This is where (4) _____ _____.

Immigration has had a profound impact on the texture of American culture. And New York City serviced as the primary entry point on the Atlantic coast for (5) _____ _____. In the late 1800s and early 1900s, millions of people emigrated from Europe to the United States to escape economic, political, and social hardships.

In 1892, the US government opened an immigration facility on Ellis Island, in New York Harbor, that processed more than 12 million people over a period of 62 years. Two-thirds of the immigrants only passed through New York on their way to other parts of the United States, while others poured into New York City, (6) _____ ____. Because they shared a common language and culture, immigrants from the same country tended to settle close together, (7) _____.

In the late nineteenth century, Chinese immigrants started to move into Lower Manhattan. Throughout the twentieth century, Chinatown continued to expand, maintaining its distinct Chinese character as New York City grew up around it. Today, (8) _____ is like a trip to the other side of the world with Chinese spoken everywhere and signs in Chinese characters. The restaurants serve unique foods, and the shops sell items from Beijing and Shanghai.

(9) _____ brought massive waves of Italians to the United States. A large percentage of these immigrants settled in the five boroughs of New York City. As the years went on, Italian neighborhoods started to disappear but one remained strong — Little Italy, (10) _____, Little Italy is a

neighborhood of restaurants, shops and businesses owned by descendants of Italian immigrants. The neighborhood is much smaller now than it used to be, but you can still walk down Mulberry Street and have a dish of flavorful pasta or a frothy cup of cappuccino.

In 1954, the immigration facility on Ellis Island closed. But the main building was later renovated and is now open as a museum and research center (11) _____. Americans can research records and ship manifests to learn when their ancestors arrived at the United States. Ellis Island is a short ferry ride from Battery Park in Manhattan and is a popular destination for both tourists and schoolchildren.

The ferry to Ellis Island also takes visitors to nearby Liberty Island to see a famous symbol of America, the Statue of Liberty. This statue, designed by sculptor Frederic-Auguste Bartholdi, was a gift from France to the United States to acknowledge the friendship established between the two countries during the American Revolution. (12) ___ _____, the Statue of Liberty towered over New York Harbor and was one of the first sights seen by immigrants when their ships sailed into the harbor.

1 ▶ Comprehension work

A Global understanding.

Read the passage carefully. Work in pairs. Fill in the blanks with the phrases from the box below. Point out the signpost language that has helped you to find the answer.

Phrases	Positions
a. creating unique neighborhoods that survive to this day	
b. just north of Chinatown and centered on Mulberry Street	
c. immigrants to the United States	
d. the first three decades of the twentieth century	
e. concentrated into a relatively small space	
f. dedicated in 1886	
g. unlike cities such as Rome or Beijing	
h. most notable the Lower East Side of Manhattan	
i. Still, with all its size and frenetic energy	
j. exploring the American immigrant experience	

| k. the buildings scrape the sky | |
| l. a walk through Chinatown | |

B Reading for highlights.

Work in pairs, write a phrase of no more than five words for each paragraph highlighting its central message.

Paragraphs	Your phrases (For reference)
1	
2	
3	
4	
5	
6	
7	
8	

2 ▶ Language work

A Learning words from their context.

Read the list of the words below, and find what word(s) serves as clues to your understanding of their meanings.

Words	Their possible meanings	Clues in the context
megalopolis		
verdant		
borough		
texture		
manifest		
cappuccino		

B Making a difference.

Answer these questions in writing.

1. What is the difference between *wilderness* and *wildness*?

2. What is the difference between *walking on the streets* and *walking the streets*?

_____

3. What is the difference between *New York City* and *the city of New York*? Are they the same thing?

_____

4. What is the difference between *service* and *serve* in this context?

_____

5. What is the difference between *immigrate* and *emigrate*?

_____

C Cloze

Fill in the blanks with suitable word.

Broadway

Broadway is exactly what its name describes — a wide avenue. It is the oldest and longest thoroughfare in the city. But Broadway is more than (1) _____ a street; it is the main artery of the American theater. People come from all over to experience the best theater the country has to (2) _____.

The term "Broadway" refers to the 32 large theaters (3) _____ around Times Square in midtown Manhattan, which is called the Theater District. Plays and musicals that are (4) _____ in a Broadway theater are considered the pinnacle of the art in America, although the productions tend to (5) _____ at mainstream audiences. The productions will (6) _____ for as long as audiences buy tickets; a show will (7) _____ when ticket sales no longer support it. This means that a Broadway (8) _____ could run for only a week or for many years, depending on its popularity. The longest running show is "The Phantom of the Opera," which opened in January 1988 and is still running today.

Off-Broadway and Off-Off-Broadway refer to New York theater productions that are (9) _____ in smaller venues scattered around the city. Off-Broadway shows are more (10) _____ than the entertainment-focused productions of Broadway. Still, productions are in established theaters with large, loyal (11) _____. Off-Off-Broadway refers to plays and (12) _____ that are alternative in form and content. The spaces in which they play are usually small theaters, or sometimes not even theaters at all. (13) _____ or outlandish productions that would never appear in Broadway or Off-Broadway theaters can find a home in Off-Off-Broadway.

PART 3 Extended Activities

1 Dictation

2 Read more

Read the passage below about the history of New York City, and then complete the tasks below.

A Potted History of New York City
By Thomas W. Santos*

There are many reasons why New York became the leading city that it is. The most compelling reason is its large, deep natural harbor. In the 1500s, European explorers marveled at the potential this protected body of water had as a seaport and trading center.

Before the Europeans arrived, the area around what is now lower New York State, New Jersey, and Delaware was inhabited by the Lenape, an Algonquin-speaking nation of hunter-gatherers. According to the history books, the first European to set eyes on New York harbor was Giovanni da Verrazano, an Italian explorer scouting the Atlantic coast of America in 1594 for the French crown. He apparently did not stay long, but the Verrazano-Narrows Bridge that connects Brooklyn and Staten Island is named for him.

The first European to map this region in earnest was the English explorer Henry Hudson. He was working for the Dutch East India Company, which had contracted him to find a trading passage to Asia by sailing west across the Atlantic. In 1609, during his exploration of the Atlantic coast, he sailed into New York Harbor and up what is now the Hudson River. He never found the passage, but the Dutch laid claim to the land he

---

* Excerpted from *New York*, published in *English Teaching Forum*, 2008. The title is added by the authors of this textbook.

had explored. In 1613, they established a fur trading post on the extreme southern end of Manhattan island and later called it New Amsterdam, also dubbing the surrounding area New Netherlands.

In 1626, Peter Minuit, the director general of the Dutch trading venture, "purchased" the whole of Manhattan from the Lenape, giving them tools, blankets and other goods in trade. It is doubtful that the Lenape saw this trade as a true purchase in the European sense, and later this clash of cultures would bring the Native Americans and the European settlers into conflict.

New Amsterdam, clinging to the southern tip of Manhattan, was not a success at first. It attracted all sorts of rough and unseemly settlers who made the little colony a fairly lawless place. In 1647, the Dutch East India Company sent a hard, humorless man named Peter Stuyvesant to clean it up. He did just that, disciplining the population and encouraging further settlement. New Amsterdam was starting to attract all sorts of people, making it a distinctly diverse place. In 1664, the British, who had formed colonies all around New Netherlands, forced the Dutch to hand over the colony. The British immediately renamed it New York. From the beginning, New York was the leading economic and cultural center of North America.

During the American Revolutionary war, the city was targeted by the British, who sent a massive war fleet into New York harbor in June to July of 1776. In late August, the British soundly defeated the revolutionary army in the Battle of Long Island. The British maintained control of New York Harbor until the end of the war.

After the United States won independence, New York was briefly the new US capital, and the first president, George Washington, was inaugurated there in 1789. But the capital was transferred to Philadelphia the following year and eventually to Washington, D.C.

In 1825, with the opening of the Erie Canal, which connected the Hudson River to the Great Lakes and opened shipping to the Midwest, New York became the premier American port on the Atlantic coast. Within 15 years, the city's population more than doubled. Over the next century, the city continued to grow, easily becoming the largest city in the New World.

In 1898, New York expanded beyond Manhattan Island when what became known as "Consolidation" was instituted. In one moment, New York City more than doubled its size and population by incorporating the boroughs of the Bronx, Queens, Brooklyn, and Staten Island. Before this historic transition, Brooklyn itself was already one of the largest cities in the country. This binding together of millions of New Yorkers was further strengthened six years later in 1904 with the opening of the New York City Subway, which made it possible to traverse the city with relative ease.

Throughout the twentieth century, New York City maintained its claim as the largest and most dynamic city in the world. As the now familiar skyline rose, American business and entertainment found in New York a fertile ground for growth. Trade and commerce, art and music, literature and journalism all thrived in this dynamic environment. And now in the twenty-first century, even as other cities in the world have become large, exciting metropolises, New York still holds a place in the world's imagination as a city where dreams can be realized, where anything is possible.

Choose the best answer to each of the following questions.

1. What did the early European explorers like about the area of New York about 500 years ago?

   A. The area was an excellent, natural harbor.

   B. The area was close to the old world.

   C. The area was rich in waterways to the inland areas.

   D. The area was full of natural marvels.

2. Who were the earliest inhabitants around what is called New York today?

   A. Italian explorers.

   B. French explorers.

   C. Native Americans.

   D. Dutch explorers.

3. What did the Dutch East India Company contract Henry Hudson to do at the beginning years of the 17th century?

   A. To produce the map of the area of New York.

   B. To produce the map of the river which was named the Hudson River later.

   C. To search for a passage to sail up the river into midland of the continent.

   D. To search for a way to the richness of Asian countries.

4. The author proposes an explanation for the conflict between the Native Americans and European settlers over the purchase of the land. What is his explanation?

   A. The Native Americans did not accept the European offer.

   B. The Native Americans did not know that the offer was made by European settlers for the purchase.

   C. The European settlers cheated the Native Americans.

   D. The European settlers did not treat the trade seriously.

5. What were the early settlers like before Peter Stuyvesant was sent to manage the southern tip of Manhattan?

   A. The area was governed by Native Americans.

   B. The area was full of lawless people.

   C. The area was well-disciplined.

   D. The area was full of law-abiding settlers.

6. What is the significance of the Battle of Long Island for the fate of New York?

   A. It marked British control over the harbor during the American War of Independence.

B. It marked the defeat of the revolutionary army.

C. It was decisive for the English to control North America.

D. It was a landmark battle for the final British defeat in North America.

7. Which of these places have been the capitals for the United States?

A. First New York, then Philadelphia, and finally Washington D.C.

B. Philadelphia, and then New York, and finally Washington D.C.

C. New Jersey, and then New York, and then Philadelphia, and finally Washington D.C.

D. New York, and then New Jersey, Philadelphia, and finally Washington D.C.

8. According to the author, the rapid growth and rise to the level of international importance of New York are attributable to one of these factors below:

A. Shipping.

B. Manufacturing.

C. Agriculture.

D. Fishing.

9. What is the actual meaning of "consolidation" in this context?

A. It means building a larger city.

B. It means a plan for building the subway system.

C. It means people can travel by subway within the city of New York.

D. It means a planning for extending New York to include other four boroughs.

10. The author concludes that today New York is _____.

A. an international city good for business and shipping.

B. a large city like any other metropolis in the world.

C. a city full of life for all kinds of people.

D. a city ideal not only for business, but also for art and education.

3 ▶ Vocabulary work

Study the following list of words, and select them to fill in the blanks of the following sentences. Make changes if you think it is necessary.

zigzag	emblem	regatta	customize	open
certificate	savor	diocese	stiff	haggle
hefty	exhilarate	veteran	pass	consecutive
panoramic	shoot	celebrate	showcase	

1. The concert hall has become an / a _____ of musical achievement for _____ performers and musicians, and has _____ the world's finest artists.

2. In this Kid's World of stuffed animals, children can _____ their stuffed friends and make an animal birth _____ .

3. The cathedral church is said to be the mother church of Episcopal _____ of New York, but its majestic doors are _____ to all visitors.

4. The lake offers magnificent views for boaters, but the service is a bit _____, and price, _____.

5. Circleboat Line provides _____ cruising experience _____ around emerald islands.

6. Skip the long ticket lines, and save 40% of admission fees at most of tourist attractions. The _____ are valid nine _____ days beginning on the date of first use. Purchase passes online or at any subway station.

7. Take a _____ vista of the city from the highest point on the top of the TV tower. High speed elevators _____ visitors up 150 meters to the top observatory in just a minute.

8. The _____ commemorates the death of the ancient Chinese poet Qu Yuan who is said to have committed suicide by drowning himself in a river to protest against the corrupted politics in his state. The boat races _____ a centuries-old Chinese tradition with a day on a narrow boat in the shape of a dragon.

9. The market is a perfect place to _____ the local flavor of food and appreciate artistic handicrafts. But don't be afraid to _____ over the prices.

C ultural Information

 Read the passage below, and then complete the task of cultural study.

United Nations Headquarters

Every year hundreds of thousands of visitors to New York City go to see the United Nations Headquarters in midtown Manhattan. The 18-acre site includes four buildings — the Secretariat, the General Assembly, the Conference building, and the Dag Hammarskjold Library. The United Nations (UN) currently has 192 members, and the flags of those nations line the plaza in front of the General Assembly Hall and Secretariat. The row of flags, displayed in English alphabetical order, from Afghanistan to Zimbabwe, stretches from 48th Street to 42nd Street.

The decision to locate United Nations Headquarters in the United States was made in 1946 by the UN General Assembly, then meeting in London. Several US locations were considered, but a donation of 8.5 million dollars from philanthropist John D. Rockefeller, Jr. secured the purchase of land at the present site. And the City of New York provided a gift of additional land. The UN complex was designed by an international team of prominent architects. American Wallace K. Harrison was named chief architect, and ten other countries each nominated an architect to the Board of Design Consultants. The 11 architects began the project in early 1947. The US government provided an interest-free loan to the United Nations for the cost of construction which began in 1949.

The Secretariat Building, which houses the UN administrative offices, was completed in 1950, and United Nations Headquarters officially opened in 1951. The Library was dedicated in 1961. Over the years, changes have been made inside the buildings to accommodate the expanded membership of the United Nations. Today the General Assembly Hall, the largest conference room, seats more than 1 800 people.

The UN Headquarters site is an international territory owned by the member nations. It has its own security force, fire department, and postal service. (The postal service issues stamps that can only be mailed from the Headquarters; tourists often mail postcards bearing these stamps.)

Taking a guided tour is the only way for visitors to see the inside of UN Headquarter. Tours are led by professional guides representing all the member nations and are conducted in many different languages. Visitors taking the tour see exhibits, various council chambers, and the General Assembly Hall. If their timing is good, they might even see a council meeting in session.

The United Nations Headquarters display many beautiful and meaningful works of art created specially for its halls and chambers. Sculptures and statues donated by member nations adorn the grounds of the complex. One sculpture, the Japanese Peace Bell, was made from the metal of coins collected from 60 different countries. Japan presented the bell to the United Nations in 1954, and it is rung every year on September 21, the International Day of Peace.

The Peace Bell and other sculptures, as well as paintings and murals inside the buildings, create an impression of grandeur and dignity, reflecting the importance of the work being done at the United Nations.

 Cultural Study Task

Study the information on United Nations' website: http://www.un.org/en/. Then write a short report on three top concerns of the United Nations now.

The Ageing Population

Introduction

In this unit, you will learn to use English for

▶ Talking about ageing population
▶ Expressing views of population ageing in writing
▶ Talking about technical issues of an ageing society

PART 1 Communicative Activities

1 Interactive listening and speaking

A Listening

In this recording, a demographic expert is discussing the population ageing in UK and Japan. Before you listen, make a guess of the possible reasons attributable to the phenomenon, and try to arrange them in order of importance.

Factors	Possible reasons for population ageing (in the order of importance)
Falling fertility rate Improved medical care Better pension system Advanced technologies Modern conveniences Increasing life expectancy Rising median age Baby boom generation	

B Choose the correct statements.

In an ageing society,

◇ Economy is different.

◇ There are more old people than the young.

◇ Young people don't like to have children.

◇ People tend to live longer than their parents.

◇ On average every woman should give birth to at least 2.2 children.

C Now, listen to the whole presentation, and take notes.

In the presentation, the expert will discuss some of the following issues. Read the list and select suitable ones for appropriate headings.

- New attitudes to being old
- Technical definition of ageing population
- Maintaining a good living standard
- Dying of rural communities
- Daily life and regular activities of the retirees
- Women's late marriage, having few children, and pursuing careers
- Flexible / optional retirement age, and the incomes
- Illnesses at an old age
- Government's pension scheme
- Burden on the adults at working age
- Health care for the retirees
- Respect-the-aged-day
- Active participation in a wide range of aspects of society
- Share of the care costs

Headings	What would it be about?
What is population ageing?	
What is their life like?	
Retirement and pensions	
Dependency ratio	
An ageing crisis in Japan	
Rising costs	

D Listening for details.

Listen to the lecture, and take notes on details.

Headings	What are the major points about this issue?
What is population ageing?	
What is their life like?	
Retirement and pensions	
Dependency ratio	
An ageing crisis in Japan	
Rising costs	

E Defining the terms.

Write explanations / definitions for the following terms.

1. population ageing

2. dependency ratio

3. compression of morbidity

4. life expectancy

5. replacement rate

6. fertility rate

_____

7. median age

_____

2 ▷ Speaking

Work in groups to make at least five suggestions for addressing population ageing in China.

● Proverb

Retirement is the ugliest expression in the world.

PART 2 Reading and Language Activities

Text   The Japanese Ageing Suit

▶ Pre-reading tasks **Discuss the following questions.**

1. Have you ever imagined what you would look like and how you would feel when you were at the age of 80?
2. What problems will an ageing population bring to society? And what preparations should and must society make to assist the elderly?

▶ Read the text

By the end of the second decade of the 21st century, almost a quarter of Japan's population will be over 65 years old. So, to help society deal with an ageing population, a Tokyo-based company has developed an "Ageing Suit". Simon Cox, a journalist of a newspaper, went along to try it out.

The few hours I spent at the "Wonderful Ageing Club", a small organization hidden away down a side street in Tokyo, were, it has to be said, rather depressing. For I was transformed, rather too quickly I thought, from a relatively healthy 36-year-old to an 80-year-old, and, dressed in the club's "ageing suit", growing old did not seem like a wonderful prospect at all.

First, I had to put on restrictive bindings to impede the movements of my main joints. Then a contraption was placed over my ankle and foot, seriously hampering my ability to move my foot independently of the rest of my leg. Similar bindings were then applied to my knees and elbows, and it was with some gratitude that, now unable to move normally, I accepted the kind offer of a walking stick. The ladies of the Wonderful Ageing Club, however, were still far from finished. Assuring me that their suit had been carefully designed on the basis of scientific research into the exact effects of ageing, they next applied a pair of special gloves to my hands to make gripping much more difficult.

Thus finished, it took me quite a few minutes before I managed to open a can of Coke — a dexterity test which, I should add, I was only able to begin after I had managed to locate the ring-pull in the first place. My vision had grown rather clouded as a result of my special glasses, which had the effects of cataracts.

A number of weights were attached to my body to create the sensation of weakened muscles, and a pair of earplugs muffled my hearing. This completed my imprisonment in a body more than twice my own age. At this point, eager to see as well as feel the effects of all this ageing engineering, I looked into a nearby mirror and found myself staring at what I can only describe as an evil in the *Star Wars* films.

There, however, any similarity with powerful science-fiction heroes, living or dead, abruptly ended. For now I found myself clumsily hobbling my way through such newly difficult tasks as going up and down stairs, sitting down on a chair and then standing up again, or reaching for things on a high shelf. Not to mention wrestling with that can of Coke or struggling, through my cataract-clouded vision, to read a newspaper.

But what is the purpose of this ageing suit? The Wonderful Ageing Club claims that it gives a very accurate representation of what being old is really like, and that, when it comes to planning for the future, that experience will be of enormous value. And people are evidently listening: about 8 000 people have tried the suit on so far, and half of them have been from local authorities, manufacturing companies or emergency service providers. They hope to see whether the products or services they offer really do meet the needs of the elderly.

Thus, throughout Japan, all kinds of products, from household appliances, to cars, to building designs, right down to the packaging in which goods are sold, are being subjected to an entirely new kind of test: they are being handled by an imitation pensioner dressed up in an ageing suit to see just how practical the products really are. No longer, it seems, is it going to be a young person's world. Not, at any rate, in the Japan of the 21st century.

Comprehension work

A Read the text again, and discuss the following questions.

1. How did the writer feel after his few hours at the "Wonderful Ageing Club"?
2. Why was the writer given a walking stick?

3. What did the ladies of the "Wonderful Ageing Club" tell the writer?
4. What was the effect of the special glasses?
5. How was the sensation of weakened muscles created?
6. What does the word "imprisonment" mean in the fourth paragraph?
7. What is the purpose and value of this ageing suit?
8. Why, in Japan, are all kinds of products being subjected to a new test? And how are they tested?

B Activity

Suppose you have experienced growing old in the "ageing suit" at the "Wonderful Ageing Club". Now, prepare a short talk about your experience with the cues in the following chart. Limit your talk to about one minute.

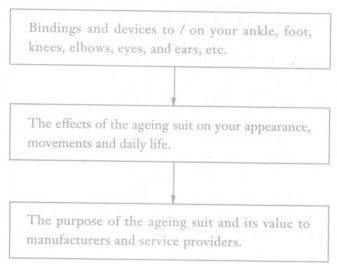

Bindings and devices to / on your ankle, foot, knees, elbows, eyes, and ears, etc.

↓

The effects of the ageing suit on your appearance, movements and daily life.

↓

The purpose of the ageing suit and its value to manufacturers and service providers.

2 ▶ Language work

A Fill in the following blanks with the words from the text.

1. The ageing suit is meant to produce a _____ of incapability of the elderly in daily life. Once a person is dressed in the suit, he will not only be totally _____ in appearance, but will also have serious _____ in his movements. Because the _____ bindings on the main _____ greatly _____ the testee's ability to move, the testee has to _____ along with the help of a walking stick.

2. Besides, various _____ are _____ to the testee's ears and eyes. His hearing is _____ by a pair of earplugs, and vision _____ by a pair of special glasses. The effect is that he cannot _____ the right thing he needs and cannot do the ordinary tasks with _____.

3. The experience of wearing the ageing suit is surely _____. But the value of the suit is _____. It enables people to see the gloomy _____ of growing old. Moreover,

it compels people to recognize the ageing population as a world-wide social problem. And finally it makes people understand what should be done for the _____.

B Rewrite the following sentences with the words and expressions in the box.

| not to mention | abruptly | wrestle | at any rate |
| apply to | grip | be subjected to | when it comes to ... |

1. To prevent insect bites, the explorers put some lotion on their skin before they entered the jungle.

   _____

2. I realized how inadequate our language could be when I was going to define a complicated idea.

   _____

3. The bill had to be put to debate in Congress.

   _____

4. I don't recall any of the bikes having a sounding device, let alone built-in lights.

   _____

5. He began to read the letter and seemed to be in deep fear and uncertainty.

   _____

6. Sade enjoyed tremendous popularity in the 80s. But in the 90s her fame as a pop singer, at least in Britain, is over.

   _____

7. The inventor ran into a difficult problem. He struggled for days to find a solution.

   _____

8. He woke up all of a sudden, as though from a nightmare.

   _____

C Word study.

   a. Give the meanings of the following words or expressions used in the text. You may use an English-English Dictionary. Then give a sentence to illustrate their meanings and usage.

   1. apply to

      _____

   2. on the basis of

      _____

   3. locate

      _____

   4. not to mention

      _____

5. be subjected to

_____

b. Each of the following clues has an example sentence. Use the prompts to produce other sentences with the same pattern as the example.

1. Prompt: binding / apply to / knee and elbow

    Example: Similar bindings were then applied to my knees and elbows.

    a. he / fall off the bike / break / leg / nurse / apply / bandage

    b. man / apply to / new paint / his house / make it look unique

    c. how much force / have to / apply to / in order to set the ball rolling

2. Prompt: suit / design / on the basis

    Example: Their suit had been carefully designed on the basis of scientific research into the exact effects of ageing.

    a. sales target / set / on the basis of / market research

    b. staff / promote / on the basis of / performance

    c. safe / predict / future / on the basis of / one opinion poll

3. Prompt: dexterity test / I / locate / ring-pull

    Example: In the dexterity test I managed to locate the ring-pull in the first place.

    a. countries / small / difficult / locate / world map

    b. operation / could not begin / until / bullet / locate / in the wound

    c. ship / locate / position / on sea / satellite

4. Prompt: I / find / clumsily hobble my way / newly difficult task / not to mention / wrestle with that can of coke

    Example: I found myself clumsily hobbling my way through such newly difficult tasks. Not to mention wrestling with that can of coke.

    a. the retarded child / difficulty / speak / mother-tongue / not to mention / learn a foreign language

    b. young man / difficulty / support / himself / not to mention / support family

    c. Madam Lin / a lot of work / not to mention / household chores

5. Prompt: throughout / Japan / products / be subjected to / test

    Example: Throughout Japan, all kinds of products are being subjected to an entirely new kind of test.

    a. English settlers / came / New World / be subjected to / hardship

    b. iron / bend / be subjected to / intense heat

    c. new theory / be subjected to / tests / before it is announced

PART 3 Extended Activities

1 Dictation

2 Read more

No one expected it to happen so quickly, and certainly not everywhere — but Homo sapiens is ageing fast. This is no bad thing, argues Fred Pearce.

The Shock of the Old*

Ushi Okushima is the oldest resident of Ogimi, the most elderly community in Japan — the country where the average age is higher than anywhere else in the world. At 108, she still takes to the floor for traditional Japanese dances. Afterwards she dabs a little French perfume behind her ears and sips the local firewater. Okushima was born when Japan had only recently seen off the shogun warlords. If an ageing population is on the way, she is not a bad advert for what we have in store.

The land of the rising sun has become the land of the setting sun with staggering speed. As recently as 1984, Japan had the youngest population in the developed world, but by 2005, it had become the world's most elderly country. Soon it will become the first country where most people are over 50 years old.

This is partly because Japanese people live longest: men can expect to reach 79 and women 86. It is also partly because Japanese have almost given up having babies: the fertility rate is just 1.2 children per woman, far lower than the 2.1 needed to maintain a steady population. The rest of the world is following Japan's example. In 19 countries, from

---

* Adapted from *New Scientist* / 27, 10 April, 2010.

Singapore to Iceland, people have a life expectancy of about 80 years. Of all the people in human history who ever reached the age of 65, half are alive now. Meanwhile, women around the world have half as many children as their mothers. And if Japan is the model, their daughters may have half as many as they do.

Homo sapiens (Latin term of "Human") is ageing fast, and the implications of this may overwhelm all other factors shaping the species over the coming decades — with more wrinkles than pimples, more walking frames than bike stabilizers, more slippers and pipes than bootees and buggies, and more grey power than student power. The longevity revolution affects every country, every community and almost every household. It promises to restructure the economy, reshape the family, redefine politics and even rearrange the geopolitical order over the coming century.

The revolution has two aspects. First, we are not producing babies like we used to. In just a generation, world fertility has halved to just 2.6 babies per woman. In most of Europe and much of East Asia, fertility is closer to one child per woman than two, way below long-term replacement levels. The notion that the populations of places such as Brazil and India will go on expanding looks misplaced: in fact, they could soon be contracting. Meanwhile, except in a handful of AIDS-ravaged countries in Africa, people are living longer everywhere.

This is frightening, even for rich nations. In Germany, France and Japan, there are fewer than two taxpaying workers to support each "Ageing may overwhelm all other factors shaping our species in the year ahead" retired pensioner. In Italy, the figure is already fewer than 1.3. Some predict that the world will face a wave of "ageing recessions".

But could there be an upside? I believe so. Flip the coin of ageing and what do we see? In 1965, The Who sang: "Hope I die before I get old." Today, those who survived drugs, binges, fast cars, or bad marriages, are older, but often still rocking and making more use of condoms than colostomy bags. Mick Jagger (born 1943) is nobody's idea of a dependant. And Tina Turner took to the stage in London, dancing in heels and a microskirt in her 70th year.

Non-celebrities also remain active, assertive and independent as they age. They fill library and seminar halls once crammed with callow and youths. They run picket lines — or marathons. Far from being a weight round society's neck, many of them look like a new human resource waiting to be tapped. Millions of the middle-class retired continue working at everything from lucrative consultancies to teaching literacy or finally finishing that PhD. They are often more valuable than the young workers who the demographers imagine are supporting them: in fact, the growing number of society's most qualified, most experienced individuals is potentially a huge demographic dividend.

In future, old people will be expected to stay in the formal economy for longer. The idea of a retirement age was invented by Otto von Bismarck in the 1880s, when as chancellor of Germany he needed a starting age for paying war pensions. He chose the age of 65 because that was typically when ex-soldiers died. But today in developed countries, and soon in poorer ones, women can expect nearly 30 years of retirement, and men 20 years.

There is a deal to be done: longer working in return for more, and more powerful, legislation to outlaw the ageism that blights the working lives of many in late middle age. The old will also expect a society that does not marginalize them; they will consider it a right to live in homes, cities and workplaces redesigned to meet their physical requirements.

Some worry that an older workforce will be less innovative and adaptable, but there is evidence that companies with a decent proportion of older workers are more productive than those addicted to youth. This is sometimes called the Horndal effect, after a Swedish steel mill where productivity rose by 15 percent as the workforce got older. Age brings experience and wisdom. Think what it could mean when the Edisons and Einsteins of the future, the doctors and technicians, the artists and engineers, have 20 to 30 more years to give us.

Of course, many older people do need healthcare, but many others are fit, competent and self-sustaining. Across Europe, typically only one retired person in 20 lives in a care home. In UK, of 10 million over-65s, just 300 000 live in care homes (that's about three per cent). So the majority of Europe's elderly resemble Okushima in Japan. They are the councilors and counselors, the social secretaries and neighborhood wardens, the carers of other elderly people, and even the political and social campaigners and agitators — the glue that holds busy societies together. Far from impoverishing societies, says John Macinnes, a demographer at the University of Edinburgh, UK, all the evidence is that "mass longevity facilitates affluence".

The "silver market" is huge. You have only to watch US network television to see the constant advertising aimed at the elderly, from Viagra and holidays to equipment and leisure wear. Oldies have savings and cash from selling large houses they no longer need. The money is available for purchases and investment — and ultimately for their children.

But this is not fundamentally society's economics of retirement. It is about society's zeitgeist, its social wellspring. The cultural historian Theodore Roszak at California State University, East Bay, once took me to task over "In developed countries, women can expect nearly 30 years of retirement" an article on the threat of ageing societies: "Ageing," he wrote, "is the best thing that has happened in the modern world, a cultural and ethical shift that looks a lot like sanity."

At 50, we do not expect to act or feel as we did at 20 — nor at 80 as we did at 50. The same is true of societies. What will it be like to live in societies that are much older than any we have known? We are going to find out, because the ageing of the human race is one of the surest predictions of this century. If the 20th century was the teenage century, the 21st will be the age of the old: it will be pioneered by the ageing baby boomers who a generation ago took the cult of youth to new heights. Without the soaring population and so many young overachievers, the tribal elders will return. More boring maybe, but wiser, surely.

The older we are, the less likely we are to be hooked on the latest gizmos and the more we should appreciate things that last. We may even reduce pressure on the world's resources by consuming less, and by conserving our environment more. We must especially hope for that, because unless the boomers can pay reparations for youthful indiscretions with the planet's limits then we may all be doomed.

The 20th century did great things. We should be proud that for the first time most children reach adulthood and most adults grow old. But after our exertions, perhaps we need to slow down a bit. Take a breather. Learn to be older, wiser and greener. Doesn't sound so bad, does it?

A Why does the writer argue that ageing is not a bad thing? What are the good things of being old? Tick the correct points below.

☐ Today, old people are still very active in both social, and personal life.

☐ One can become a good example to see off the times of shogun warlords in Japan.

☐ One can live longer, but has lower fertility.

☐ Old women are allowed to wear make-up, and spray perfume.

☐ One is still independent even tough one's old today.

☐ Old age is a new human resource just as useful as the youth.

☐ One gets marginalized in society when one gets old.

☐ Wisdom on the basis of age is a source of wealth.

☐ Society is stronger in solidarity with old people.

☐ Old age is a new area with great potential of market value.

☐ A society with aged people is more reasonable in thinking.

☐ A society with a lot of old people is boring.

☐ Old people are more conservative in trying out new ideas and products.

☐ A society with old people will consume less environmental resources.

☐ We should pride on ourselves on our great achievement of surviving the times of war, disasters, and diseases in the 20th century.

B The article is characterized by the creative, metaphorical, and colorful use of language. Recast the ideas in the creative use of language in your own words.

1. The land of the rising sun has become the land of the setting sun with staggering speed.

_____

2. Homo sapiens is ageing fast, and the implications of this may overwhelm all other factors shaping the species over the coming decades—with more wrinkles than pimples, more walking frames than bike stabilizers, more slippers and pipes than bootees and buggies, and more grey power than student power.

_____

3. But could there be an upside? I believe so. Flip the coin of ageing and what do we see?

_____

4. Today, those who survived drugs, binges, fast cars, or bad marriages, are older, but often still rocking and making more use of condoms than colostomy bags.

_____

5. They are the councilors and counselors, the social secretaries and neighborhood wardens, the carers of other elderly people, and even the political and social campaigners and agitators — the glue that holds busy societies together.

_____

6. It is about society's zeitgeist, its social wellspring.

_____

7. ... the ageing baby boomers who a generation ago took the cult of youth to new heights. Without the soaring population and so many young overachievers, the tribal elders will return.

_____

8. The older we are, the less likely we are to be hooked on the latest gizmos and the more we should appreciate things that last.

_____

9. We must especially hope for that, because unless the boomers can pay reparations for youthful indiscretions with the planet's limits then we may all be doomed.

_____

3 ▶ Grammar work

Correct the mistakes in the use of the passive voice or past perfect of the verbs in the following passage.

Two men tried to sell a painting that had been stolen. The painting had been owned by Mainmi Gillies, aged 84. She said it had presented to one of her ancestors by the artist. She had owned it since 1926, when it had been given to her as a wedding present. One of the men, Mr. X, who cannot name for legal reasons, was found suspicious because he was looking for a buyer. He told a police detective, who disguised as a wealthy art lover, he was willing to sell the painting cheap because it was stolen. A meeting had then arranged at an airfield near Retford, where the painting was to be flown in and exchanged, but the airfield was staffed by police officers in plain clothes. Mr. X arrived at the airfield with another man. They showed the money in a suitcase. The buyer had then been taken to see the painting in a barn. Mr. X was arrested but Mr. Henry who had come with Mr. X was escaped.

4 Word formation

Fill in the following blanks with the words in the box.

heat	dirty	wrong	must	round
final	breakfast	dear	better	right

1. If you _____ the building, you will see a workshop.
2. The sun _____ and brings life to the earth.
3. The local government endeavored to _____ the situation.
4. The little baby is really a _____.
5. You should know how to make a distinction between _____ and _____.
6. Memorizing vocabulary is a _____ in learning a foreign language.
7. Boys tend to _____ their clothes while playing.
8. Our team got all the way through to the _____.
9. They _____ at the youth hostel.

> *Conversion* is a process by which a word belonging to one word class is used as part of another word class without the addition of an affix. Words produced by conversion are mainly nouns, verbs, or adjectives: for example, ***a swim*** (*v⇒n*), ***to holiday*** (*n⇒v*), ***average*** (*n⇒adj*). Words of other classes can also be converted to nouns or verbs: for instance, You said too many ***ifs*** and ***buts***. (*conj⇒n*); *Please **forward** the letter to Professor White.* (*adv⇒v*)

5 Vocabulary work

A What is ageing like?

Which of the following symptoms could be related to ageing?

1. Tom felt dizzy after working overnight.
2. Jo is breathless after half an hour's walk to the station.
3. Liz had a bad cold. She was shivery when she was waiting for the bus.
4. Paul coughed a lot recently. Probably he was down with the flu.
5. Rose had a stomachache. But her doctor said it was not a big deal.
6. Alf said, "If you are my age, you will also feel bad at night."
7. Sam had to admit that he often felt tired and should not work so hard.
8. Anne felt rather stressed. She had to take a good holiday.
9. Perry has had painful joints for many years. And recently, they have got worse.

B What do doctors do?

Fill in the blanks with the words from the word box.

measure	take	listen to	further	questions
look in	examine	pressure	feel	

They (1) _____ your temperature, (2) _____ your pulse, (3) _____ your chest, (4) _____ your ears, (5) _____ you, take your blood (6) _____, ask you some (7) _____ and weigh and (8) _____ you before sending you to a big hospital for (9) _____ tests.

6 ▶ Translation

Put the following sentences into English.

1. 仅凭一次调查就得出的结论是否可靠？ **on the basis of**
2. 为了满足老龄社会的需要，将有更多的有关体育锻炼的书籍出版。**meet the needs of**
3. 队长要求队员们无论如何要打赢这场足球赛。 **at any rate**
4. 他游览过世界上许多的名胜，更不用提国内的景点了。**not to mention**
5. 科学家对新产品做了一系列严格的测试。**subject to**
6. 他在房间里搜索了一阵，找出了一堆旧杂志。**bring out**
7. 她下决心要取得成功，什么也挡不住她。**get in one's way**
8. 吉米的父母从美国过来看他。**come over**

7 ▶ Writing

Comment briefly on the following remarks.

1. To be young again is the dream of most old people.

   _____

2. The evening light is immeasurably sweet. Only the yellow dusk is approaching too fast!

   _____

3. Wisdom grows in proportion to age.

   _____

4. If beard means wisdom, the goat is to be respected.

   _____

5. The dearest worship for the dead is not as valuable as a peanut offered to the alive.

   _____

Cultural Information

Read the passage below, and then complete the task of cultural study.

Age and Sex Structures in UK and US

Although the total population in Britain has remained relatively stable in the last decade, there have been noticeable changes in the age and sex structure, including a decline in the proportion of young people under 16 and an increase in the proportion of elderly people, especially those aged 85 and over. Now, over 20 per cent of the population are over the normal retirement ages (65 for men and 60 for women), compared with 15 per cent in the early 1960s.

According to the statistics in the late 80s, there were an estimated 29.3 million females and 27.8 million males in Britain, representing a ratio of over 105 females to every 100 males. There are about 5 per cent more male than female births every year. Because of the higher mortality of men at all ages, however, there is a turning point, at about 48 years of age, at which the number of women exceeds the number of men. This imbalance increases with age so that there are many more women among the elderly.

The same situation is found in the United States. Estimated in June, 1996, there were 129.5 million males and 135.6 million females, of which 33.5 million were over 65 of age.

 Cultural Study Task

Study the articles posted on the Internet on the issues of China's population. Write an essay in about 300 words on the challenges we face, and the strategies we are taking to address them. Comment if these strategies are effective based on your observation.

Key to Phonetic Symbols

RP symbols (consonants)	Examples	RP symbols (vowels)	Examples
p	pen	ɪ	kit
b	back	e	dress
t	ten	æ	cat
d	day	ɒ	dog (*BrE*)
k	key	ʌ	cut
g	get	ʊ	put
f	fat	ə	about
v	view	i	happy
θ	thing	u	actuality
ð	then	iː	sheep
s	soon	ɑː	father
z	zero	ɒː	dog (*AmE*)
ʃ	ship	ɔː	four
ʒ	pleasure	uː	boot
h	hot	ɜː	bird
x	loch	eɪ	make
tʃ	cheer	aɪ	lie
dʒ	jump	ɔɪ	boy
m	sum	əʊ	mote (*BrE*)
n	sun	oʊ	note (*AmE*)
ŋ	sung	aʊ	now
w	wet	ɪə	real
l	let	eə	hair (*BrE*)
r	red	ʊə	sure (*BrE*)
j	yet	uə	actual
		ɪə	peculiar

Special Signs

BrE / *AmE* means British English / American English

/ˈ/ shows main stress

/ˌ/ shows secondary stress

/◄/ shows stress shift

/ˈⁱ/ means that some speakers use /ɪ/ and some use /ə/

/ə/ means that /ə/ may or may not be used

(Based on *Longman Dictionary of Contemporary English*, ©Longman Group UK Limited, 2003)

郑重声明

高等教育出版社依法对本书享有专有出版权。任何未经许可的复制、销售行为均违反《中华人民共和国著作权法》，其行为人将承担相应的民事责任和行政责任，构成犯罪的，将被依法追究刑事责任。为了维护市场秩序，保护读者的合法权益，避免读者误用盗版书造成不良后果，我社将配合行政执法部门和司法机关对违法犯罪的单位和个人给予严厉打击。社会各界人士如发现上述侵权行为，希望及时举报，本社将奖励举报有功人员。

反盗版举报电话　（010）58581897/58581896/58581879

反盗版举报传真　（010）82086060

E-mail　dd@hep.com.cn

通信地址　北京市西城区德外大街 4 号　高等教育出版社打击盗版办公室

邮编　100120

购书请拨打电话　（010）58581118

出版物数码防伪说明

本图书采用出版物数码防伪系统，用户购书后刮开封底防伪密码涂层，将 16 位防伪密码发送短信至106695881280，免费查询所购图书真伪，同时您将有机会参加鼓励使用正版图书的抽奖活动，赢取各类奖项，详情请查询中国扫黄打非网（http://www.shdf.gov.cn）。

反盗版短信举报

编辑短信"JB，图书名称，出版社，购买地点"发送至 10669588128

数码防伪客服电话

（010）58582300/58582301

网络学习平台使用说明

1. 英语专业四八级考试平台由权威命题专家根据考试大纲编写开发，系统针对考生答案自动评分，每套试题均配有详尽解析，请登录网址：http://exam.cflo.com.cn；

2. 登录方法：请使用本书封底标签上防伪明码作为登录账号，防伪密码作为登录密码；

3. 注意事项：账号有效学习时间为激活后 1 年，激活后可享用两次免费考试机会。

电子邮箱　cflo_tem@pub.hep.cn

咨询电话　4008122365

图书在版编目（CIP）数据

综合英语教程 . 2/邹为诚主编 . —3 版 . —北京：高等教育出版
社，2011.5
学生用书
ISBN 978-7-04-031754-1

Ⅰ.①综… Ⅱ.①邹… Ⅲ.①英语－高等学校－教材 Ⅳ.① H31

中国版本图书馆 CIP 数据核字（2011）第 055326 号

总 策 划	刘 援	策划编辑	贾 巍	项目编辑	甘红娜	责任编辑	李 瑶
封面设计	张 志	版式设计	刘 艳 魏 亮	责任校对	甘红娜	责任印制	朱学忠

出版发行	高等教育出版社	网　　址	http://www.hep.edu.cn
社　　址	北京市西城区德外大街 4 号		http://www.hep.com.cn
邮政编码	100120	网上订购	http://www.landraco.com
印　　刷	涿州市星河印刷有限公司		http://www.landraco.com.cn
开　　本	850×1168　1/16		
印　　张	15.5	版　　次	1998 年 12 月第 1 版
字　　数	389 000		2011 年 5 月第 3 版
购书热线	010-58581118	印　　次	2011 年 5 月第 1 次印刷
咨询电话	400-810-0598	定　　价	35.00 元（含光盘）

本书如有缺页、倒页、脱页等质量问题，请到所购图书销售部门联系调换。
版权所有　侵权必究
物 料 号　31754-00